"The cookbook **Bearly Any Fat Too**, like its predecessor **Bearly Any Fat**, has been reviewed by The Obesity Foundation Board and we believe it is an excellent source to enhance weight reduction and weight maintenance."

The Obesity Foundatin, a non-profit organization whose mission statement is: to prevent, to control, and ultimately cure the disease of obesity by providing in-depth education to health professionals and the general public, and to support selective research projects on the cause, course, effects, and treatment of obesity.

James F. Merker. CAE
Executive Director
The Obesity Foundation

A special thank you to Judy Pellow, R.D., M.S., for her help in completing the nutrient analysis of the recipes in this cookbook. She did a wonderful job in my first cookbook and I enjoyed working with her on this endeavor. Judy is a former member of the Board of Directors for the Obesity Foundation.

Sheri Dunn
Author/Illustrator

In the following pages you will find low fat, low salt and low sugar recipes which are quick and easy to prepare. In addition to healthier eating, remember to add some form of exercise to your day.

ENJOY THE RECIPES!!

ENJOY THE BEARS!!

ENJOY LIFE!!

©Recipes and Illustrations by Sheri Dunn, copyright

This cookbook is dedicated to my friends and family, and those of you who are enjoying my first cookbook, "Bearly Any Fat". Without your help, support and encouragement, this second cookbook would not have been possible.

A warm and sincere thank you to you all.

A special thank you to my husband, Greg, and my daughter, Crystal, for their patience, encouragement and love.

Since I first started working on this second cookbook, great progress has been made in the nutritional contents of several foods on the market. Make sure that you read and understand the labels. DON'T BE FOOLED!!

Please feel free to substitute some of the new fat-free and salt-free foods as you see fit.

ABBREVIATIONS USED IN THIS COOKBOOK:

- c - cup
- T - tablespoon
- t - teaspoon
- lb. - pound
- oz. - ounce

TABLE OF CONTENTS

BEANS AND SOUPS -------------------------------------- 1- 16

BREADS AND MUFFINS --------------------------------- 17- 36

DESSERTS -- 37- 66

DIPS, DRESSINGS AND SAUCES ---------------------- 67- 80

EXTRAS -- 81-102

FISH AND POULTRY ------------------------------------ 103-142

PASTA, POTATOES AND RICE ---------------------- 143-166

SALADS -- 167-184

INDEX --- 185-190

ORDERING INFORMATION ------------------------- 191-192

BEANS & SOUPS

BAKED BEANS

Combine in casserole dish:
- 1 (15 oz.) chili beans (no meat)
- 1 T apple juice, undiluted
- 1 T ketchup
- 1/2 c chopped onion
- 1 t Dijon mustard
- 1 (7 1/2 oz.) crushed unsweetened pineapple

Cover and bake at 350° for 20 minutes. Sprinkle with:
- 1 T brown sugar

Bake, uncovered, for 10 more minutes. Serves 6.

Calories per serving: 107

Carbohydrates: 22 g Fiber: 4.7 g
Protein: 4 g Sodium: 312 mg
Cholesterol: 0 mg
Total Fat: < 1 g
Saturated Fat: 0 g
Monounsaturated Fat: .1 g

Calories from protein: 16%
Calories from carbohydrates: 81%
Calories from fats: 3%

BAKED BEANS WITH APPLE

In bowl combine:
- 1 c black beans, cooked
- 1 c pinto beans, cooked
- 1/4 c molasses
- 1/4 c ketchup
- 2 T vinegar
- 1/2 t dry mustard
- 1/2 t salt
- 1/4 c apple juice, undiluted

Sliced into thin slices:
- 1 med. purple onion

Layer bean mixture, alternately with onion rings, in casserole dish. Top with:
- 2 apples, thinly sliced

Bake, uncovered, for 45 to 60 minutes at 325°. Serves 6.

Calories per serving: 160

Carbohydrates:	35 g	Fiber:	6.7 g
Protein:	6 g	Sodium:	302 mg
		Cholesterol:	0 mg
Total Fat:	< 1 g		
Saturated Fat:	.1 g		
Monounsaturated Fat:	.1 g		

Calories from protein: 13%
Calories from carbohydrates: 84%
Calories from fats: 3%

BLACK BEAN CHILI

In crockpot place:
- 3 (15 oz.) cans black beans, rinsed and drained
- 2 T cumin seeds
- 2 T oregano
- 2 c finely chopped onions
- 1 c finely chopped green pepper
- 1/2 c finely chopped red pepper
- 1 1/2 T paprika
- 1 t ground pepper
- 1/2 t minced garlic
- 1 can (28 oz.) stewed tomatoes
- 1/3 c canned jalapeno peppers
- 1 to 2 c water

Cook on low for 4 to 6 hours. Serves 16.

Calories per serving: 131

Carbohydrates: 25 g   Fiber: 8.4 g
Protein: 8 g   Sodium: 121 mg
Cholesterol: 0 mg
Total Fat: < 1 g
Saturated Fat: .1 g
Monounsaturated Fat: .1 g

Calories from protein: 23%
Calories from carbohydrates: 71%
Calories from fats: 6%

BLACK BEAN AND RICE SALAD

Mix in large bowl:
    1 c brown rice, cooked and cooled
    1 can (11 oz.) corn
      (no salt or sugar added)
    1 can (15 oz.) black beans,
      rinsed and drained
    1/2 c chopped green pepper
    1/2 c chopped tomato

Arrange on lettuce leaves on individual salad plates. Top each salad with:
    1 T salsa

Serves 6.

Calories per serving: 167

    Carbohydrates: 34 g   Fiber: 7.9 g
    Protein: 8 g   Sodium: 18 mg
        Cholesterol: 0 mg

    Total Fat: 1 g
      Saturated Fat: .2 g
    Monounsaturated Fat: .4 g

    Calories from protein: 17%
    Calories from carbohydrates: 77%
    Calories from fats: 6%

ANASAZI BEAN SOUP

In crockpot combine:
    1 sm. chopped onion
    1 lb. uncooked Anasazi beans
    8 c water

Cook on high until beans are firm. Then add:
    1 t garlic powder
    1 c smoked turkey breast, chopped
    1 (14 1/2 oz.) can stewed tomatoes
      (low-salt)
    1 (11 oz.) can Mexican corn
    1/2 t pepper
    1/2 t Spike (all-purpose spice)

Cook until beans are tender. Serves 12.

Calories per serving: 179

Carbohydrates:	31 g	Fiber:	3.2 g
Protein:	13 g	Sodium:	20 mg
		Cholesterol:	8 mg

Total Fat: 1 g
    Saturated Fat: .2 g
    Monounsaturated Fat: .2 g

Calories from protein: 28%
Calories from carbohydrates: 66%
Calories from fats: 6%

BLACK BEAN SOUP

In crockpot place:
- 1 can (15 oz.) black beans, rinsed
- 2 c water
- 2 t low-salt chicken instant granules
- 1 med. onion, chopped
- 3 cloves garlic, finely chopped
- 1 T molasses
- 1 T vinegar
- 3 T salsa
- 1 can (14 1/2 oz.) stewed tomatoes (low-salt)
- 1/2 c frozen corn
- 1/2 t Spike (all-purpose seasoning)

Cook for 2 to 3 hours on low until thoroughly heated. Add more water, if necessary. Serves 6.

Calories per serving: 125

Carbohydrates:	25 g	Fiber:	7.9 g
Protein:	7 g	Sodium:	121 mg
		Cholesterol:	0 mg
Total fat:	1 g		
Saturated Fat:	.1 g		
Monounsaturated Fat:	.2 g		

Calories from protein: 20%
Calories from carbohydrates: 75%
Calories from fats: 6%

Chicken Noodle Soup

Sauté in pan sprayed with vegetable spray until chicken is tender:
- 1 lb. chicken breast, cubed
- 1 med. onion, chopped

In crockpot place:
- 2 c salt-free, fat-free chicken broth
- 3 c water
- 1 c carrots, chopped
- 1 c celery, sliced
- 1/2 c red pepper, chopped
- 1/2 c green pepper, chopped
- 1/2 t pepper
- 1/4 t thyme
- 1 t salt-free Italian Blend spice
- 1/2 t salt
- 1 t salt-free lemon herb spice

Add chicken mixture and cook on low until vegetables are tender, 2 to 3 hours. Add:
- 2 c cooked pasta

Simmer 30 more minutes. Add more water, if necessary. Serves 10.

Calories per serving: 100

- Carbohydrates: 3 g
- Protein: 15 g
- Fiber: .1 g
- Sodium: 157 mg
- Cholesterol: 38 mg
- Total Fat: 2 g
- Saturated Fat: .1 g
- Monounsaturated Fat: .1 g

- Calories from protein: 64%
- Calories from carbohydrates: 13%
- Calories from fats: 23%

FRENCH ONION SOUP

In large saucepan sauté:
- 4 c thinly sliced yellow onions
- 1 c thinly sliced white onions
- 1 T diet margarine
- 1/2 t ground black pepper

Cook, stirring frequently with a wooden spoon, until onions are a light brown color. Sprinkle onions with:
- 1 T unbleached flour

Stir until flour disappears. Cook for 1 more minute, stirring constantly. Remove from heat.

In bowl dissolve:
- 2 T low-sodium beef bouillon
- 1 t salt
- 3 c hot water

Gradually add beef broth to onion mixture, stirring constantly. Return to medium-high heat and bring mixture to a boil. Add:
- 3 c water
- 1 bay leaf

Bring to boil. Reduce heat to low and cook, uncovered, for 30 to 40 minutes. Discard bay leaf.

When ready to serve, place soup into individual, broilerproof soup bowls and then onto a jelly roll pan. On top of each bowl place:
- 1 slice toasted French bread (6 slices)
- 3/4 c grated lowfat mozzarella cheese, divided between the 6 bowls

Broil until cheese melts and turns golden. Remove from oven; serve immediately. Serves 6.

(Continued Next Page)

French Onion Soup (Continued)

Calories per serving: 243

Carbohydrates:	31 g	Fiber:	3.2 g
Protein:	13 g	Sodium:	750 mg
		Cholesterol:	15 mg
Total Fat:	7 g		
Saturated Fat:	3.7 g		
Monounsaturated Fat:	2.2 g		

Calories from protein: 21%
Calories from carbohydrates: 51%
Calories from fats: 27%

Gazpacho

In large bowl combine:
- 1 (46 oz.) can tomato juice (low-salt)
- 1 med. onion, finely chopped
- 2 lg. tomatoes, chopped
- 1 green pepper, finely chopped
- 1 cucumber, peeled, seeded *and* diced
- 2 scallions, minced
- 1 clove garlic, crushed
- 1/4 c fresh parsley, chopped
- 2 T olive oil
- 2 T lime juice
- 2 T red wine vinegar
- 1 1/2 T lemon juice
- 1 t dried whole tarragon
- 1 t basil
- 1 t honey
- 1/2 t salt
- 1/4 t pepper
- 1/4 t ground cumin
- Dash of hot sauce

Stir well. Chill at least 2 hours before serving. Makes 9 cups.

Calories per serving: 73

Carbohydrates:	11 g	Fiber:	2.4 g
Protein:	2 g	Sodium:	137 mg
		Cholesterol:	0 mg

Total Fat: 3 g
Saturated Fat: .5 g
Monounsaturated Fat: 2.2 g

Calories from protein: 9%
Calories from carbohydrates: 55%
Calories from fats: 36%

Mexican Bean Soup

In large crockpot place:
- 1 1/2 c chopped onions
- 1 1/2 t minced garlic
- 1 can (16 oz.) stewed tomatoes (no salt added)
- 1 c zucchini, chopped
- 1 can (16 oz.) black beans, rinsed and drained
- 1 can (16 oz.) kidney beans, rinsed and drained
- 2 c water
- 1 can (4 oz.) chopped green chilies
- 2 t chili powder
- 1 t whole cumin seeds
- 1/2 t dried oregano
- 1/2 t salt

Add more water, if necessary. Cook on low for 6 to 8 hours. Serves 12.

Calories per serving: 101

Carbohydrates:	19 g	Fiber:	6.8 g
Protein:	6 g	Sodium:	101 mg
		Cholesterol:	0 mg

Total Fat: < 1g
Saturated Fat: .1 g
Monounsaturated Fat: .1 g

Calories from protein: 23%
Calories from carbohydrates: 72%
Calories from fats: 5%

Pea Soup

Soak overnight:
    2 c split green peas

In crockpot place:
    Peas, drained
    1 c carrots, grated
    1 c celery, chopped
    1 1/2 c onion, chopped
    1 lg. clove garlic
    2 c cabbage, finely chopped
    10 c water
    1 t basil
    1 t thyme
    1 t marjoram
    1/2 t oregano
    1/4 t sage
    1 vegetable bouillon (low-salt)
    4 T fresh parsley

Cook over medium-high heat for 6 to 8 hours or until peas are cooked thoroughly. Serves 16.

Calories per serving: 41

Carbohydrates: 8 g   Fiber: 2 g
Protein: 2 g   Sodium: 16 mg
    Cholesterol: 0 mg

Total Fat: < 1 g
Saturated Fat: 0 g
Monounsaturated Fat: 0 g

Calories from protein: 23%
Calories from carbohydrates: 74%
Calories from fats: 4%

POTATO SOUP

Place in large saucepan:
> 5 med. potatoes, washed, unpeeled and chopped
> 1 c onion, chopped
> 1 c celery, chopped
> 1/4 c celery leaves, chopped

Bring to boil. Continue to cook until potatoes are tender. Drain, reserving liquid. Using hand potato masher, gently mash vegetable mixture. Return mixture to pan and add:
> 2 c skim milk
> 1 1/2 c reserved liquid
> 1 t beef bouillon granules (low-sodium)
> 1/2 t salt
> 1 T chopped chives

Continue to cook on medium heat until thoroughly heated. Serves 10.

Calories per serving: 132

Carbohydrates: 29 g   Fiber: 2.6 g
Protein: 4 g   Sodium: 96 mg
Cholesterol: < 1 mg
Total Fat: < 1 g
Saturated Fat: .1 g
Monounsaturated Fat: 0 g

Calories from protein: 13%
Calories from carbohydrates: 85%
Calories from fats: 2%

Quick Soup

In skillet sprayed with vegetable spray sauté:
- 3/4 lb. ground turkey breast
- 1/2 c chopped onion
- 1/2 c chopped green pepper

In large pot add:
- 2 cans (14 1/2 oz.) Italian style stewed tomatoes
- 1 can (15 oz.) mixed vegetables
- 2 c water
- 2 t instant chicken granules (low-sodium)
- 1/2 t oregano
- Turkey mixture
- 1/2 c uncooked noodles (yolkless)

Cook until thoroughly heated and noodles are tender. Serves 12.

Calories per serving: 96

Carbohydrates:	13 g	Fiber:	3.3 g
Protein:	9 g	Sodium:	80 mg
		Cholesterol:	15 mg
Total Fat:	1 g		
Saturated Fat:	.3 g		
Monounsaturated Fat:	.2 g		

Calories from protein: 37%
Calories from carbohydrates: 52%
Calories from fats: 12%

VEGETABLE BARLEY SOUP

In crockpot place:
- 1 c onion, chopped
- 1 c carrot, chopped
- 1 c celery, sliced
- 6 c water
- 1 can (28 oz.) stewed tomatoes (low-sodium)
- 1 can (16 oz.) black beans, rinsed and drained
- 1 c frozen corn
- 1 c green pepper, chopped
- 1 c frozen green peas
- 1 T basil
- 3 chicken bouillon cubes (low-salt)
- 1 t pepper
- 1 t garlic powder

Cook on medium heat 2 to 3 hours or until vegetables are tender, then add:
- 1 c quick cooking barley
- 1/2 t salt

Continue to cook until barley is tender. Serves 14.

Calories per serving: 106

Carbohydrates:	22 g	Fiber:	6.4 g
Protein:	5 g	Sodium:	108 mg
		Cholesterol:	0 mg
Total Fat:	< 1 g		
Saturated Fat:	.1 g		
Monounsaturated Fat:	.1 g		

Calories from protein: 19%
Calories from carbohydrates: 76%
Calories from fats: 4%

BREADS, MUFFINS & ROLLS

CHERRY BANANA BREAD

In small bowl whip:
- 2 egg whites
- 1/3 c apple juice concentrate
- 1 t cherry extract
- 1/4 c skim milk

Add:
- 1 1/2 c unbleached flour
- 1/2 c whole wheat flour
- 1 t baking soda
- 1/2 t cinnamon
- 1/4 t salt
- 1/4 t nutmeg
- 2 T chopped cherries

Mix until well-blended, then add:
- 1 c mashed bananas
- 2 T sugar

Mix well. Pour into 2 small loaf pans (7 1/2 x 3 1/2 inch) sprayed with vegetable spray and lightly floured. Bake at 350° for 30 to 35 minutes, until done. Makes 14 slices.

Calories per serving: 101

Carbohydrates: 22 g Fiber: 1.3 g
Protein: 3 g Sodium: 108 mg
Cholesterol: 0 mg
Total Fat: > 1 g
Saturated Fat: < 1 g
Monounsaturated Fat: 0 g

Calories from protein: 11%
Calories from carbohydrates: 86%
Calories from fats: 3%

CRANBERRY BREAD

In small bowl combine:
- 2 egg whites
- 1/3 c orange juice, undiluted
- 1/4 c water
- 1 t grated orange rind
- 3/4 c sugar
- 2 T melted diet margarine

Mix until well-blended. Set aside. In large bowl combine:
- 2 c unbleached flour
- 1 3/4 t baking powder
- 1/2 t salt
- 1/2 t baking soda
- 1/2 t coriander

Make a well in the dry ingredients and add the orange mixture. Stir and add:
- 2 c fresh cranberries, chopped
- 1/3 c chopped walnuts

Mix well. Pour into 2 bread pans sprayed with vegetable spray. Bake at 350° for 45 to 50 minutes or until done. Makes 2 loaves. Serves 24.

Calories per serving: 83

Carbohydrates:	16 g	Fiber:	.7 g
Protein:	2 g	Sodium:	102 mg
		Cholesterol:	0 mg
Total Fat:	2 g		
Saturated Fat:	.1 g		
Monounsaturated Fat:	.4 g		

Calories from protein: 8%
Calories from carbohydrates: 76%
Calories from fats: 16%

EASY RAISIN BREAD

In bowl mix:
>2 c whole wheat flour
>1 c unbleached flour
>2 t baking soda
>1/4 t salt
>1 t cinnamon

Add:
>1/2 c molasses
>2 c skim milk
>2 T vinegar

Mix until well-blended. Fold in:
>1 c raisins

Pour into 2 (3 1/2 x 7 inch) loaf pans sprayed with vegetable spray and lightly floured. Let stand for 45 minutes. Bake at 325° for 30 to 35 minutes or until done. Makes 20 slices.

Calories per serving: 114

Carbohydrates:	26 g	Fiber:	2 g
Protein:	3 g	Sodium:	120 mg
		Cholesterol:	0 mg
Total Fat:	< 1 g		
Saturated Fat:	.1 g		
Monounsaturated Fat:	< 1 g		

Calories from protein: 11%
Calories from carbohydrates: 86%
Calories from fats: 3%

Jalapeno Corn Bread

In small bowl mix:
- 1 c cornmeal
- 1 c skim milk
- 1 T lemon juice

In large bowl combine:
- 1 c unbleached flour
- 1 T sugar
- 1 t baking powder
- 1 t baking soda
- 2 egg whites
- 1 T light olive oil

Mix until well-blended. Add cornmeal mixture. Stir. Add:
- 1 can (8 3/4 oz.) corn, drained
- 1 to 2 T jalapeno peppers
- 1 c lowfat cheddar cheese, grated

Pour into 13 x 9 inch pan sprayed with vegetable spray. Bake at 375° for 25 to 30 minutes, until done. Cut into squares. Serves 12.

Calories per serving: 143

Carbohydrates: 22 g   Fiber: 1.7 g
Protein: 6 g   Sodium: 234 mg
Cholesterol: 5 mg
Total Fat: 3 g
Saturated Fat: 1.3 g
Monounsaturated Fat: 1.5 g

Calories from protein: 18%
Calories from carbohydrates: 61%
Calories from fats: 22%

PUMPKIN BREAD

In bowl combine:
- 1/4 c brown sugar
- 1 c skim milk
- 3 T molasses
- 2 egg whites
- 1/2 c applesauce
- 3/4 c pumpkin (canned, unsweetened)

Stir until well-blended, then add:
- 1 c whole wheat flour
- 1/2 c unbleached flour
- 1/2 c cornmeal
- 1/2 t baking soda
- 1/2 t baking powder
- 1 T cinnamon
- 1/2 t nutmeg

Pour into bread pan sprayed with vegetable spray. Bake at 350° for 40 to 45 minutes or until done. Serves 12.

Calories per serving: 123

Carbohydrates:	22 g	Fiber:	2 g
Protein:	4 g	Sodium:	71 mg
		Cholesterol:	0 mg
Total Fat:	<1 g		
Saturated Fat:	.1 g		
Monounsaturated Fat:	.06 g		

Calories from protein: 12%
Calories from carbohydrates: 73%
Calories from fats: 3%

Pumpkin Date Bread

In bowl combine:
- 1 c canned pumpkin
- 3 egg whites
- 2 T diet margarine
- 1/4 c applesauce
- 3 T brown sugar
- 1/2 c buttermilk

Using whisk, beat until blended. Add:
- 1 c whole wheat flour
- 1/2 c unbleached flour
- 1 t baking powder
- 1 t baking soda
- 1 t cinnamon
- 1/2 t nutmeg
- 1/4 t cloves
- 1/4 t allspice

Mix well. Add:
- 1 c reg. oats, uncooked
- 1/2 c chopped dates

Spray 2 loaf pans (7 1/2 x 4 inch) with vegetable spray. Pour batter into pans. Bake at 350° for 45 to 50 minutes, until done. Serves 12.

Calories per serving: 139

Carbohydrates:	28 g	Fiber:	2.7 g
Protein:	5 g	Sodium:	145 mg
		Cholesterol:	0 mg
Total Fat:	2 g		
Saturated Fat:	.4 g		
Monounsaturated Fat:	.6 g		

Calories from protein: 13%
Calories from carbohydrates: 76%
Calories from fats: 11%

BANANA BLUEBERRY MUFFINS

In bowl combine:
    2 egg whites
    1/2 c apple juice, undiluted
    2 med. mashed bananas

Add:
    1 c unbleached flour
    1/2 c whole wheat flour
    1/2 c oat bran
    1/2 t cinnamon
    1/2 t lemon peel
    1 T baking powder
    1/2 t baking soda
    3 T sugar

Mix well, then fold in:
    1 c fresh or frozen blueberries

Pour into prepared muffin pan and bake at 400° for 12 to 15 minutes or until done. Makes 12 muffins.

Calories per serving: 103

    Carbohydrates: 23 g   Fiber: 2 g
        Protein: 3 g   Sodium: 127 mg
                           Cholesterol: 0 mg
        Total Fat: < 1 g
            Saturated Fat: .1 g
        Monounsaturated Fat: .1 g

        Calories from protein: 11%
    Calories from carbohydrates: 86%
            Calories from fats: 4%

Banana Oatmeal Muffins

In bowl combine:
    1 c mashed ripe bananas
    1 egg white
    1/4 c apple juice, undiluted
    1 t cherry extract
    1 T sugar

Add:
    1/2 c oatmeal
    1 t baking soda
    1/2 t cinnamon
    1/4 t coriander
    1 c unbleached flour
    2 T skim milk

Stir until well-blended, then add:
    1/2 c raisins

Spoon into muffin pan sprayed with vegetable spray. Bake at 375° for 15 minutes or until done. Makes 12 muffins.

Calories per serving: 97

Carbohydrates: 22 g   Fiber: 1.6 g
Protein: 2 g   Sodium: 75 mg
Cholesterol: 0 mg
Total Fat: <1 g
Saturated Fat: .1 g
Monounsaturated Fat: .1 g

Calories from protein: 9%
Calories from carbohydrates: 87%
Calories from fats: 4%

BANANA RAISIN NUT MUFFINS

In large bowl combine:
>1 T diet margarine
>1 T raspberry juice, undiluted
>1 egg white
>2 T brown sugar
>1 c skim milk
>3/4 c mashed ripened bananas

Add:
>1 c unbleached flour
>1/2 c whole wheat flour
>1/2 c oat bran
>1 t baking powder
>1/4 t baking soda
>1 t cinnamon

Mix well. Add:
>2 T crushed walnuts
>1/2 c raisins

Mix well. Pour into muffin pan sprayed with vegetable spray. Bake at 375° for 12 minutes or until done. Makes 14 muffins.

Calories per serving: 119

Carbohydrates: 24 g Fiber: 2 g
Protein: 3 g Sodium: 63 mg
Cholesterol: 0 mg
Total Fat: 2 g
Saturated Fat: .3 g
Monounsaturated Fat: .5 g

Calories from protein: 11%
Calories from carbohydrates: 77%
Calories from fats: 12%

BLUEBERRY MUFFINS

In bowl combine:
- 1 c skim milk
- 2 egg whites
- 1/4 c brown sugar
- 3 T apple juice

Add:
- 1/2 c unbleached flour
- 1 c uncooked oats
- 1 T baking powder
- 1/2 t cinnamon

Mix until well-blended, then fold in:
- 1 c fresh or frozen blueberries

Pour into muffin pan sprayed with vegetable spray. Bake at 400° for 15 minutes or until done. Makes 12 muffins.

Calories per serving: 82

Carbohydrates:	16 g	Fiber:	1 g
Protein:	3 g	Sodium:	104 mg
		Cholesterol:	0 mg
Total Fat:	< 1 g		
Saturated Fat:	1 g		
Monounsaturated Fat:	2 g		

Calories from protein: 14%
Calories from carbohydrates: 79%
Calories from fats: 6%

Carrot Muffins

In bowl whip:
    1 c skim milk
    2 egg whites
    2 t lemon juice
    2 t pineapple juice
    3 T brown sugar

Add:
    1 c whole wheat flour
    1/2 c unbleached flour
    1 t baking powder
    1/2 t baking soda
    1/4 t salt
    1/2 t cinnamon
    1/4 c bran flakes

Mix well, then add:
    1 1/2 c grated carrot
    1/2 c chopped dates

Pour into muffin pan sprayed with vegetable spray. Bake at 400° for 15 minutes. Makes 12 muffins.

Calories per serving: 106

Carbohydrates:	23 g	Fiber:	2 g
Protein:	4 g	Sodium:	141 mg
		Cholesterol:	0 mg
Total Fat:	< 1 g		
Saturated Fat:	.1 g		
Monounsaturated Fat:	.1 g		

Calories from protein: 13%
Calories from carbohydrates: 84%
Calories from fats: 3%

Mandarin Orange Muffins

In large bowl whip with fork:
>2 egg whites
>1/2 c mandarin orange juice, drained from can
>1/4 c orange juice, diluted
>2 T sugar
>1/2 t almond extract
>1/2 t orange extract

Add:
>1 T wheat germ
>1 c unbleached flour
>1/2 t baking soda
>1/2 t baking powder
>1/4 t ground cloves

Mix until well-blended. Then add:
>1/2 c mandarin oranges, halved

Pour into prepared muffin pan. Bake at 350° for 15 to 20 minutes. Makes 12 muffins.

Calories per serving: 59

Carbohydrates:	13 g	Fiber:	.5 g
Protein:	2 g	Sodium:	57 mg
		Cholesterol:	0 mg
Total Fat:	<1 g		
Saturated Fat:	0 g		
Monounsaturated Fat:	0 g		

Calories from protein: 12%
Calories from carbohydrates: 85%
Calories from fats: 2%

ORANGE-RASPBERRY MUFFINS

In bowl combine:
- 2 T apple juice
- 2 T diet margarine
- 1/2 c orange juice, diluted
- 3 egg whites

Add:
- 1 1/2 c unbleached flour
- 1/4 c sugar
- 1/4 c brown sugar
- 2 t baking powder

Fold in:
- 3/4 c fresh or thawed raspberries
- 3 t fresh grated orange peel

Mix well. Pour into prepared muffin pan. Bake at 375° for 15 to 20 minutes, until done. Makes 12 muffins.

Calories per serving: 116

Carbohydrates:	24 g	Fiber:	1 g
Protein:	3 g	Sodium:	93 mg
		Cholesterol:	0 mg
Total Fat:	1 g		
Saturated Fat:	.2 g		
Monounsaturated Fat:	.4 g		

Calories from protein: 9%
Calories from carbohydrates: 82%
Calories from fats: 9%

Pineapple Muffins

In large bowl whip with whisk until frothy:
- 2 egg whites
- 1/2 c pineapple juice, undiluted
- 3 T sugar
- 1 t cherry extract

Add:
- 1 1/2 c unbleached flour
- 1/2 t soda
- 1/2 t baking powder
- 1/8 t salt
- 1/2 t cinnamon
- 1/4 t cloves

Stir and then add:
- 1 c crushed pineapple, drained (unsweetened)

Pour into prepared muffin pan. Bake at 350° for 18 to 20 minutes or until done. Makes 12 muffins.

Calories per serving: 91

Carbohydrates:	20 g	Fiber:	1 g
Protein:	2 g	Sodium:	79 mg
		Cholesterol:	0 mg
Total Fat	< 1 g		
Saturated Fat:	0 g		
Monounsaturated Fat:	0 g		

Calories from protein: 10%
Calories from carbohydrates: 88%
Calories from fats: 2%

Pumpkin Muffins

In bowl combine:
- 2 egg whites
- 1 t vanilla
- 1 c pumpkin
- 8 packets Sweet 'N Low

Add:
- 2/3 c dry nonfat milk
- 6 T flour
- 2 t pumpkin pie spice
- 1 t cinnamon
- 1 t baking soda

Mix well. Fold in:
- 1/4 c raisins
- 1/2 c grated carrots

Pour into muffin pan sprayed with vegetable spray. Bake at 350° for 15 minutes or until done. Makes 12 muffins.

Calories per serving: 50

Carbohydrates:	10 g	Fiber:	1 g
Protein:	3 g	Sodium:	100 mg
		Cholesterol:	< 1 g
Total Fat:	0 g		
Saturated Fat:	0 g		
Monounsaturated Fat:	0 g		

Calories from protein: 21%
Calories from carbohydrates: 77%
Calories from fats: 3%

Tangerine Muffins

In bowl mix with fork:
- 1 c skim milk
- 1 T vinegar
- 2 T Pure & Light mandarin-tangerine juice, undiluted
- 1 T grated tangerine peel
- 2 egg whites
- 1 T diet margarine

Mix until blended, then add:
- 1 3/4 c unbleached flour
- 1/4 c sugar
- 1/4 t salt
- 1 T baking soda
- 1/2 t coriander
- 1 c raisins

Drop into muffin pan sprayed with vegetable spray. Bake at 375° for 15 to 20 minutes. Makes 12 muffins.

Calories per serving: 139

Carbohydrates:	30 g	Fiber:	2 g
Protein:	4 g	Sodium:	282 mg
		Cholesterol:	0 mg
Total Fat:	1 g		
Saturated Fat:	.2 g		
Monounsaturated Fat:	.2 g		

Calories from protein: 10%
Calories from carbohydrates: 85%
Calories from fats: 5%

Applesauce Rolls

In bowl mix with fork:
- 2 egg whites
- 1 c applesauce (unsweetened)
- 1/4 c molasses

Add:
- 2 c unbleached flour
- 3 t baking powder
- 1 1/2 t cinnamon
- 1/4 t cloves
- 1 c chopped apples

Drop by spoon onto prepared cookie sheet. Bake at 375° for 12 minutes. Makes 18 rolls.

Calories per serving: 76

Carbohydrates: 17 g   Fiber: 1 g
       Protein: 2 g   Sodium: 62 mg
                       Cholesterol: 0 mg
Total Fat: 0 g
    Saturated Fat: 0 g
Monounsaturated Fat: 0 g

Calories from protein: 10%
Calories from carbohydrates: 88%
Calories from fats: 2%

BISCUITS

In bowl mix:
    2 c unbleached flour
    1/4 t salt
    1/2 t cream of tartar
    1 t sugar
    2 T baking powder
    1/4 c plus 1 T nonfat dry milk

Add and mix with fork:
    1/4 c diet margarine

Add 3/4 cup plus 1 tablespoon water (add more water, if necessary).

Drop by spoon into a hot skillet sprayed with vegetable spray. Cook on low, turning biscuits as they cook. Cook 10 to 15 minutes or until done. Makes 12 biscuits.

Calories per serving: 102

Carbohydrates:	18 g	Fiber:	.6 g
Protein:	3 g	Sodium:	264 mg
		Cholesterol:	0 mg
Total Fat:	2 g		
Saturated Fat:	.4 g		
Monounsaturated Fat:	.7 g		

Calories from protein: 11%
Calories from carbohydrates: 70%
Calories from fats: 18%

Oat Bran Biscuits

In small bowl mix:
>1/4 c oat bran
>3/4 c buttermilk

Let stand.

In mixing bowl combine:
>1 1/3 c unbleached flour
>1 1/2 t baking powder
>1/2 t baking soda
>1/4 t salt
>3 T diet margarine

Add bran mixture to flour mixture. Form into ball and place on floured surface. Roll dough to 1/2 inch thickness. Cut into 2 inch round biscuits. Bake at 425° for 12 minutes. Makes 12 biscuits.

Calories per serving: 83

Carbohydrates:	14 g	Fiber:	.6 g
Protein:	3 g	Sodium:	170 mg
		Cholesterol:	< 1 g
Total Fat:	2 g		
Saturated Fat:	.4 g		
Monounsaturated Fat:	.7 g		

Calories from protein: 12%
Calories from carbohydrates: 67%
Calories from fats: 21%

QUICK BISCUITS

In large bowl combine:
        3 1/2 c unbleached flour
        1/4 t salt
        1/2 t baking soda
        1/4 c sugar
        2 t baking powder

In small bowl combine:
        1 c buttermilk
        1 T diet margarine, melted
        1 pkg. yeast, dissolved in
            1/2 c warm water

Add liquid mixture to flour mixture. Add additional flour, if needed. Shape dough lightly into 24 balls. (Handle dough as little as possible.) Place balls into cake pans sprayed with vegetable spray. Bake at 400° for 15 minutes or until done. Makes 24 biscuits.

Calories per serving: 82

Carbohydrates: 17 g   Fiber: .5 g
Protein: 2 g   Sodium: 84 mg
                 Cholesterol: < 1 mg
Total fat: < 1 g
        Saturated Fat: .1 g
    Monounsaturated Fat: .1 g

Calories from protein: 12%
Calories from carbohydrates: 83%
Calories from fats: 6%

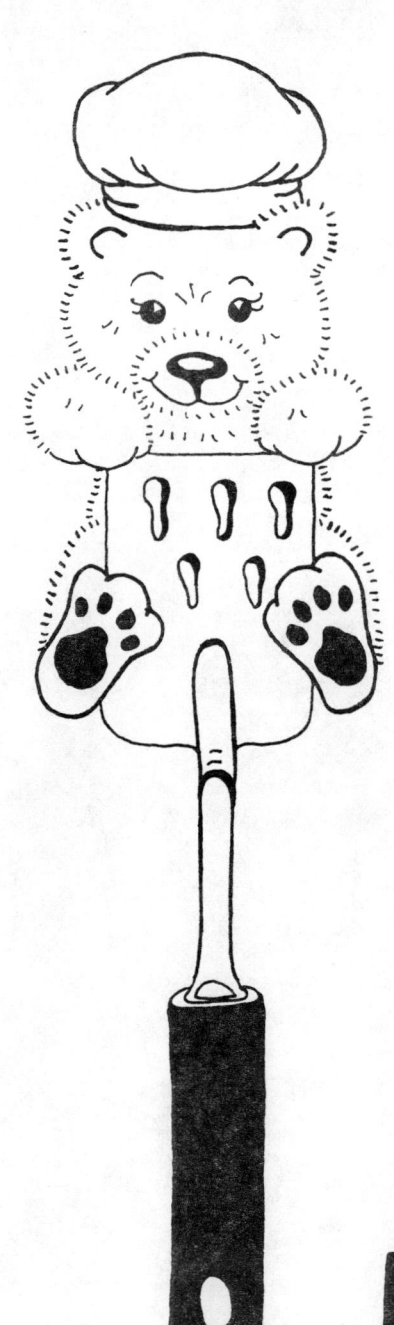

DESSERTS

Apple-Butterscotch Bars

In a large bowl stir:
> 1/4 c apple juice, undiluted
> 1/2 c brown sugar
> 1/2 c applesauce
> 1 t vanilla
> 1 egg white

Add:
> 1 1/4 c unbleached flour
> 1 t baking soda
> 1 t cinnamon
> 1/4 t cloves

Stir until blended. Add:
> 1 c finely chopped apple
> 1/2 c raisins
> 1/3 c butterscotch morsels
> 1/2 c oatmeal

Spread into prepared 11 x 7 x 2 inch pan. Bake at 350° for 20 minutes or until done. Makes 16.

Calories per serving: 208

Carbohydrates:	41 g	Fiber:	3 g
Protein:	6 g	Sodium:	61 mg
		Cholesterol:	0 mg
Total Fat:	3 g		
Saturated Fat:	1 g		
Monounsaturated Fat:	1 g		

Calories from protein: 11%
Calories from carbohydrates: 77%
Calories from fats: 12%

Apple Tart

In bowl place:
>1 1/2 c unbleached flour
>1 t baking powder

Cut in using pastry blender or fork:
>1/2 c diet margarine

Blend until mixture resembles coarse crumbs. Add:
>3 T ice water
>1 T lemon juice

Stir until dough holds together. Add additional water, if necessary. Form dough into a ball. Place on floured surface. Roll out into a 13 inch round. (Edges can be uneven.)

Transfer dough to sideless cookie sheet sprayed lightly with vegetable spray.

Core, peel, halve and slice into thin slices:
>4 medium apples

Leaving a 2 inch border, arrange apples in concentric circles from outside toward middle. Sprinkle with the following.

In small bowl combine:
>1/3 c sugar
>1/2 t nutmeg
>1 t cinnamon

Sprinkle sugar mixture over apples. Fold edges of pastry over apples (apples in middle will be exposed).

(Continued Next Page)

Apple Tart (Continued)

Bake at 375° for 35 to 45 minutes, until apples are tender and pastry is golden. Cool on wire rack. Serves 8.

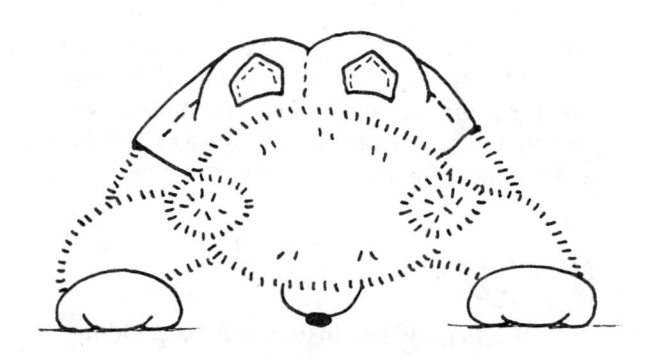

Calories per serving: 205

Carbohydrates: 36 g   Fiber: 2.2 g
Protein: 3 g   Sodium: 178 mg
Cholesterol: 0 mg
Total Fat: 6 g
Saturated Fat: 1.2 g
Monounsaturated Fat: 2.2 g

Calories from protein: 5%
Calories from carbohydrates: 69%
Calories from fats: 26%

BANANA CREAM PIE

In food processor place:
    14 graham cracker halves

Blend until finely chopped. Makes 1 1/4 cups.

In bowl add:
    1 c finely chopped graham cracker crumbs
    1/2 c oatmeal flakes
    1/4 c finely chopped almonds
    1 egg white, beaten
    1/2 t cinnamon

Mix well. Pour into pie plate sprayed with vegetable spray. Using the back of a spoon, press mixture into pie plate. If mixture sticks to spoon, wet spoon with water. Bake at 350° for 6 to 8 minutes. Cool.

PIE FILLING:
In bowl add:
    2 pkgs. (9 oz.) instant banana pudding (sugar-free)
    2 1/2 c (1%) lowfat milk
    1/2 c lowfat vanilla yogurt

With whisk, whip for 1 to 2 minutes, until blended. Add:
    3 med. bananas, sliced

Mix thoroughly. Pour into chilled pie crust. Sprinkle with remaining 1/4 cup graham cracker crust.

Chill at least 1 hour before serving. Serves 8.

(Continued Next Page)

BANANA CREAM PIE (CONTINUED)

Calories per serving: 195

Carbohydrates: 31 g
Protein: 8 g
Fiber: 3 g
Sodium: 167 mg
Cholesterol: 4 mg

Total Fat: 5 g
Saturated Fat: 1.4 g
Monounsaturated Fat: 2.3 g

Calories from protein: 15%
Calories from carbohydrates: 62%
Calories from fats: 22%

Banana Orange Cookies

In large bowl combine:
      1 1/2 c mashed ripened bananas
      1/4 c diet margarine
      1/2 c applesauce
      1/2 c orange juice, undiluted
      2 egg whites
      2 t vanilla
      1 t grated orange peel

Add:
      1 1/2 c unbleached flour
      3/4 t baking soda
      2 1/2 c rolled oats
      1/2 t nutmeg
      1/4 t ground cloves

Mix well, then add:
      3/4 c raisins

Spray a cookie sheet with vegetable spray. Drop mixture by spoon onto cookie sheet. Bake at 350° for 12 to 15 minutes or until done. Cool. In small bowl combine:
      3/4 c powdered sugar
      5 t orange juice
      1 t grated orange peel

After cookies are cooled, drizzle frosting mixture over them. Makes 2 1/2 dozen. Serving size = 1 cookie.

(Continued Next Page)

BANANA ORANGE COOKIES
(CONTINUED)

Calories per serving: 93

Carbohydrates:	19 g	Fiber:	1 g
Protein:	2 g	Sodium:	43 mg
		Cholesterol:	0 mg

Total Fat: 1 g
  Saturated Fat: .3 g
  Monounsaturated Fat: .5 g

Calories from protein: 9%
Calories from carbohydrates: 78%
Calories from fats: 12%

BANANA PUDDING PIE

Line bottom and sides of 9 inch pie plate with:
    30 vanilla wafer cookies (rounded sides up, overlapping on sides as necessary)

In bowl whisk:
    2 pkgs. (3 1/2 oz.) vanilla instant pudding
    3 c skim milk

Pour half of mixture into cookie crust. Peel and cut into thin slices:
    2 med. bananas

Place bananas in small bowl and sprinkle with:
    Juice of 1 sm. lemon

Arrange half of bananas on top of pie filling in crust. Pour remaining filling over bananas. Top with remaining bananas. Refrigerate at least 30 minutes.

Swirl over top of pie:
    1 c lite Cool Whip, thawed

Serves 8.

Calories per serving: 187

Carbohydrates:	30 g	Fiber:	.7 g
Protein:	5 g	Sodium:	178 mg
		Cholesterol:	14 mg
Total Fat:	6 g		
Saturated Fat:	3.3 g		
Monounsaturated Fat:	.8 g		

Calories from protein: 10%
Calories from carbohydrates: 61%
Calories from fats: 28%

BUTTERMILK-CINNAMON COFFEE CAKE

In bowl combine:
- 2 c unbleached flour
- 1/2 c brown sugar
- 1/4 c sugar
- 1 T cinnamon
- 1/4 t ginger
- 1/4 t nutmeg
- 1 t baking soda
- 1 t baking powder

In small bowl combine:
- 1/4 c orange juice, undiluted
- 1 c buttermilk
- 2 egg whites

Pour liquid mixture into flour mixture. Stir until blended. Pour into 13 x 9 inch baking pan sprayed with vegetable spray. In small bowl combine:
- 1/2 c unbleached flour
- 2 T brown sugar
- 1 t cinnamon
- 1 T finely chopped walnuts

Sprinkle over cake batter. Bake at 350° 30 to 35 minutes or until done. Serves 16.

Calories per serving: 130

Carbohydrates:	28 g	Fiber:	.7 g
Protein:	3 g	Sodium:	99 mg
		Cholesterol:	< 1 mg
Total Fat:	< 1 g		
Saturated Fat:	.1 g		
Monounsaturated Fat:	.1 g		

Calories from protein: 9%
Calories from carbohydrates: 86%
Calories from fats: 5%

CHEWY DATE BARS

In bowl combine:
- 2/3 c whole wheat flour
- 1/4 c brown sugar
- 1/4 c sugar
- 1 t cinnamon
- 1/3 c oatmeal
- 1 c chopped dates

In small bowl beat:
- 1 egg yolk
- 2 egg whites

Pour egg mixture over flour mixture and mix with fork. Batter will be thick.

Spray 9 inch square pan with vegetable spray. Press mixture into pan. Bake at 350° for 20 to 25 minutes or until done. Makes 8 bars.

Calories per serving: 168

Carbohydrates:	39 g	Fiber:	3 g
Protein:	3 g	Sodium:	18 mg
		Cholesterol:	33 mg
Total Fat:	1 g		
Saturated Fat:	.3 g		
Monounsaturated Fat:	.5 g		

Calories from protein: 8%
Calories from carbohydrates: 86%
Calories from fats: 6%

CHOCOLATE-AMARETTO CHEESECAKE

In 8 inch square pan sprinkle:
    6 chocolate wafers (lowfat), finely crushed

In food processor place:
    1 1/2 c lowfat cream cheese
    3/4 c sugar
    1 c (1 %) lowfat cottage cheese
    1/4 c plus 2 T unsweetened cocoa
    1/4 c unbleached flour
    1/4 c amaretto
    1 t vanilla

Process until smooth, then add:
    1 egg white, beaten

Process until smooth, then fold in:
    2 T semi-sweet chocolate morsels

Pour mixture over crumbs in pan. Bake at 300° for 45 to 50 minutes or until cheesecake is set. Let cool in pan on wire rack. Cover and chill for at least 8 hours. Serves 12.

Calories per serving: 172

Carbohydrates:	19 g	Fiber:	.3 g
Protein:	6 g	Sodium:	185 mg
		Cholesterol:	21 mg

Total Fat: 7 g
Saturated Fat: 4.4 g
Monounsaturated Fat: 2.2 g

Calories from protein: 14 %
Calories from carbohydrates: 46 %
Calories from fats: 40 %

HERSHEY'S FUDGE CAKE

In bowl combine:
- 1/4 c diet margarine
- 2 T apple juice, undiluted
- 3/4 c sugar
- 3 egg whites
- 1 t vanilla
- 2 pkgs. Sweet 'N Low

With mixer, beat until light and fluffy. In small bowl blend to make smooth paste:
- 1/3 c Hershey's cocoa
- 1/4 c plus 2 to 3 T hot water

Gradually add cocoa mixture to the creamed mixture. Add:
- 3/4 c skim milk
- 1 T vinegar

Mix well. Add:
- 1 3/4 c unbleached flour
- 1 t baking powder
- 1 t baking soda

Mix well. Pour into 13 x 9 inch pan sprayed with vegetable spray. Bake at 350° for 20 to 30 minutes or until done.

FROSTING:
In small bowl add:
- 1 1/2 c powdered sugar
- 1/8 t unsweetened cocoa
- 1/4 c diet margarine
- 1 t vanilla
- 2 T skim milk

Beat with mixer until creamy. Add more milk, if necessary. Frost cooled cake.

(Continued Next Page)

HERSHEY'S FUDGE CAKE (CONTINUED)

Calories per serving: 174

Carbohydrates: 34 g   Fiber: .5 g
Protein: 3 g   Sodium: 168 mg
Cholesterol: 0 mg
Total Fat: 3.5 g
Saturated Fat: .8 g
Monounsaturated Fat: 1 g

Calories from protein: 7%
Calories from carbohydrates: 76%
Calories from fats: 18%

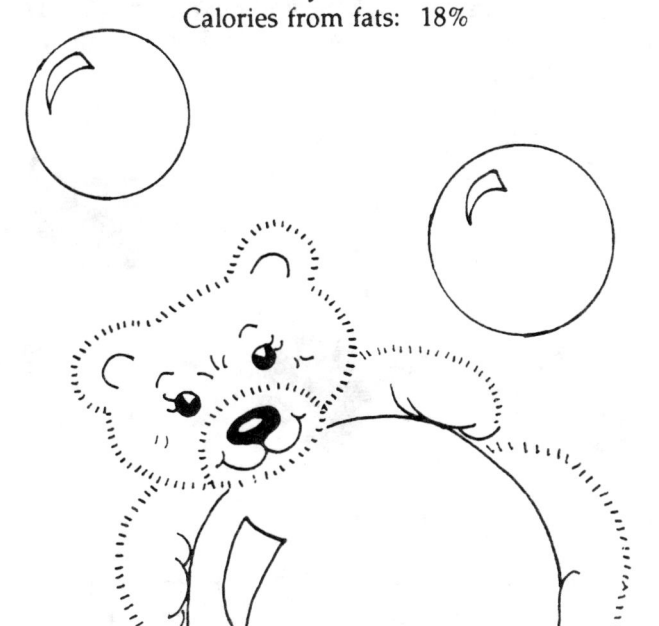

INSTANT SORBET

Freeze in can:
> 1 can (20 oz.) crushed pineapple (packed in own juice)

Thaw pineapple enough to remove it from the can; cut into chunks. Put in food processor along with:
> 1 c fresh or frozen raspberries
> 1 c strawberries, sliced
> 2 peaches, peeled and cubed

Process until pureed. Spread mixture into 8 x 8 inch pan and freeze solid. Thaw slightly before serving.

Scoop into dishes. Serves 6.

Calories per serving: 87

Carbohydrates:	22 g	Fiber:	3.3 g
Protein:	1 g	Sodium:	1 mg
		Cholesterol:	0 mg
Total Fat:	< 1 g		
Saturated Fat:	0 g		
Monounsaturated Fat:	0 g		

Calories from protein: 4%
Calories from carbohydrates: 93%
Calories from fats: 3%

JELL-O CAKE

In bowl mix with blender:
- 1/4 c diet margarine
- 1/4 c applesauce
- 1/3 c lemon Jell-O (sugar-free)
- 2 T sugar
- 1 t lemon extract

Beat until light and fluffy. In small bowl combine:
- 2 c unbleached flour
- 2 1/2 t baking powder
- 1/4 c nonfat dry milk

Add flour mixture to Jell-O mixture. Mix well. Fold in:
- 1 c skim milk
- 1/4 c mandarin juice, drained from can

Gently fold in:
- 3 egg whites, beaten until stiff
- 1 can (11 oz.) mandarin oranges, drained

Pour batter in 13 x 9 inch pan sprayed with vegetable spray. Bake at 350° for 25 to 30 minutes, until center springs back.

Cool on wire rack. Serves 12.

Dust with powdered sugar if you would like.

(Continued Next Page)

JELL-O CAKE (CONTINUED)

Calories per serving: 144

Carbohydrates: 25 g Fiber: 1.5 g
Protein: 6 g Sodium: 149 mg
Cholesterol: 0 mg
Total Fat: 2 g
Saturated Fat: .4 g
Monounsaturated Fat: .8 g

Calories from protein: 18%
Calories from carbohydrates: 69%
Calories from fats: 13%

MICROWAVE CARAMEL CORN

Place in brown paper grocery bag:
    16 c. popped corn
        (not buttered or salted)

Place in bowl:
    1 c brown sugar
    1/4 c light Karo syrup
    1/2 c diet margarine
    1 t salt

Microwave on high 1 to 2 minutes. Stir Microwave 3 more minutes and add:
    1/2 t baking soda
    1 t vanilla

Stir and pour immediately over popcorn. Place bag in microwave for 1 minute on high. Shake well. Microwave 1 more minute and shake for 30 seconds. Microwave for 30 more seconds. Shake well. Pour onto cookie sheets. Separate corn and let cool. Makes 16 cups. Serving size - 1 cup.

Calories per serving: 121

Carbohydrates:	23 g	Fiber:	1.5 g
Protein:	1 g	Sodium:	211 mg
		Cholesterol:	0 mg
Total Fat:	3 g		
Saturated Fat:	.6 g		
Monounsaturated Fat:	1.3 g		

Calories from protein: 3%
Calories from carbohydrates: 74%
Calories from fats: 23%

OATMEAL COOKIES

In bowl combine:
> 2 T diet margarine
> 2 T frozen apple juice, undiluted
> 1/4 c applesauce
> 1/2 c brown sugar
> 1/4 c sugar
> 2 egg whites
> 1 t vanilla

Mix well. Add:
> 1 c whole wheat flour
> 1 t baking soda
> 1 t cinnamon
> 1/2 t nutmeg
> 1/4 t cloves
> 1/2 c crushed cornflakes

Mix well. Fold in:
> 2 c quick cooking oats
> 1/2 c raisins
> 1 c finely chopped apple

Spray cookie sheet with vegetable spray. Drop dough by teaspoon onto cookie sheet. Bake at 350° for 8 to 10 minutes. Makes 4 1/2 dozen. Serving size = 1 cookie.

Calories per serving: 42

Carbohydrates: 9 g
Protein: 1 g
Fiber: .7 g
Sodium: 27 mg
Cholesterol: 0 mg
Total Fat: < 1 g
Saturated Fat: .1 g
Monounsaturated Fat: .2 g

Calories from protein: 9%
Calories from carbohydrates: 81%
Calories from fats: 10%

OATMEAL BUTTERSCOTCH COOKIES

In bowl combine:
- 1/4 c diet margarine
- 1/4 c applesauce
- 1/4 c brown sugar
- 1/4 c sugar
- 3 egg whites
- 1/4 c molasses
- 1 t maple extract

Add:
- 1 c unbleached flour
- 1 t cinnamon
- 1/2 t baking soda
- 2 1/2 c quick cooking oats

Mix well, then fold in:
- 1 c butterscotch chips

Spray cookie sheet with vegetable spray. Drop dough by teaspoon onto cookie sheet. Bake at 350° for 8 to 10 minutes or until done. Makes 60 cookies. Serving size = 1 cookie.

Calories per serving: 35

Carbohydrates: 6 g   Fiber: .3 g
Protein: 1 g   Sodium: 19 mg
                      Cholesterol: 0 mg
Total Fat: < 1 g
    Saturated Fat: .1 g
    Monounsaturated Fat: .2 g

Calories from protein: 11%
Calories from carbohydrates: 74%
Calories from fats: 15%

ORANGE-OAT-CHOC COOKIES

In bowl combine:
>1/4 c diet margarine
>1/2 c brown sugar
>1/2 c applesauce
>1/2 c sugar
>3 egg whites
>2 T skim milk
>1 t vanilla
>1 t orange extract
>1 T grated orange peel

Beat until mixture is creamy. Add:
>1 1/2 c unbleached flour
>1 t baking soda
>1 t cinnamon
>1/4 t cloves

Fold in:
>2 1/2 c Quaker Oats

Mix well. Fold in:
>1 c semi-sweet chocolate morsels

Drop by spoon onto cookie sheet sprayed with vegetable spray. Bake at 375° for 8 to 10 minutes. Makes 5 dozen.

Calories per serving: 57

Carbohydrates:	10 g	Fiber:	.4 g
Protein:	1 g	Sodium:	27 mg
		Cholesterol:	0 mg
Total Fat:	2 g		
Saturated Fat:	.7 g		
Monounsaturated Fat:	.6 g		

Calories from protein: 8%
Calories from carbohydrates: 67%
Calories from fats: 25%

Peach Cobbler

In bowl combine:
- 1/2 c brown sugar
- 1/2 t cinnamon
- 1 t grated lemon rind
- 1 T lemon juice

Add:
- 4 c sliced peeled peaches

Toss to mix. Place in 8 x 8 inch baking dish sprayed with vegetable spray. Bake at 375° for 8 minutes. In bowl combine:
- 1/4 c diet margarine
- 1/4 c sugar
- 2 egg whites
- 1/2 c skim milk
- 1 t vanilla

Beat until fluffy. Add:
- 3/4 c unbleached flour
- 1/2 c whole wheat flour
- 1 T baking powder

Drop batter by spoonfuls over peach mixture; spread gently. Bake at 375° for 25 to 30 minutes, until top is golden brown. Serves 8.

Calories per serving: 297

Carbohydrates:	62 g	Fiber:	3.3 g
Protein:	4 g	Sodium:	227 mg
		Cholesterol:	0 mg
Total Fat:	3 g		
Saturated Fat:	.6 g		
Monounsaturated Fat:	1 g		

Calories from protein: 6%
Calories from carbohydrates: 85%
Calories from fats: 9%

Peanut Butter Cookies

In mixing bowl combine:
  1/3 c unsweetened applesauce
  1/2 c chunky peanut butter
  1/3 c brown sugar
  1/2 c sugar
  2 egg whites
  1 t vanilla extract

Beat with electric mixer until well-blended. Then add:
  3/4 c unbleached flour
  1/4 c whole wheat flour
  1 t cinnamon

Beat with mixer just until blended. Stir in with spoon:
  1/4 c unbleached flour

Drop by teaspoon onto cookie sheet lightly sprayed with vegetable spray. Bake at 350° for 8 to 10 minutes. Do not over cook. Makes 36 cookies.

Calories per serving: 56

Carbohydrates:	9 g	Fiber:	.5 g
Protein:	2 g	Sodium:	18 mg
		Cholesterol:	0 mg
Total Fat:	2 g		
Saturated Fat:	.3 g		
Monounsaturated Fat:	.9 g		

Calories from protein: 12%
Calories from carbohydrates: 59%
Calories from fats: 29%

PUMPKIN CHIFFON PIE

In bowl combine:
- 1 1/2 c crushed gingersnaps
- 1/4 c diet margarine
- 1 T apple juice, undiluted
- 1/4 c powdered sugar

Press firmly into pie plate. Chill for several hours.

In saucepan combine:
- 1/2 c sugar
- 1 1/4 c pumpkin
- 1/2 c skim milk
- 1/2 t ginger
- 1/2 t cinnamon

Cook until thickened. Dissolve:
- 1 T gelatin
- 1/4 c cold water

Let stand for 5 minutes. Add to pumpkin mixture. Mix and cool. In bowl place:
- 3 egg whites
- 1/4 c sugar

Beat with mixer until stiff. Fold egg whites into pumpkin mixture. Pour into pie crust and chill. Serves 8.

(Continued Next Page)

PUMPKIN CHIFFON PIE (CONTINUED)

Calories per serving: 237

Carbohydrates: 44 g Fiber: 3 g
Protein: 5 g Sodium: 237 mg
Cholesterol: 0 mg
Total Fat: 5 g
Saturated Fat: 1.3 g
Monounsaturated Fat: 2.1 g

Calories from protein: 8%
Calories from carbohydrates: 73%
Calories from fats: 19%

QUICK PUDDING DELIGHT

In bowl whip until set:
    1 pkg. (3 oz.) instant banana pudding
    1 c skim milk

Fold in:
    4 oz. lowfat Cool Whip
    3/4 c mandarin oranges, drained,
      reserving liquid
    1/4 c mandarin juice
    2/3 c crushed pineapple, drained
    1 banana, sliced

Serve into dishes and refrigerate for at least 30 minutes. Serves 6.

Calories per serving: 174

Carbohydrates:	34 g	Fiber:	1.3 g
Protein:	5 g	Sodium:	277 mg
		Cholesterol:	12 mg
Total Fat:	3 g		
Saturated Fat:	2 g		
Monounsaturated Fat:	1 g		

Calories from protein: 10%
Calories from carbohydrates: 74%
Calories from fats: 17%

RAISIN BARS

In bowl combine:
      1/3 c brown sugar
      1 egg white
      1 t lime peel, grated
      1 T lime juice
      1/2 c skim milk
      2 T apple juice, undiluted
      1 T diet margarine

Add:
      1 c unbleached flour
      1/2 t baking powder
      1/4 t baking soda

Fold in:
      1/2 c raisins

Spread evenly in a 12 x 7 1/2 inch baking dish sprayed with vegetable spray. Bake at 350° for 20 to 25 minutes or until done. Let cool, then frost with the following.

In small bowl combine:
      1 c powdered sugar
      1 T lime juice
      1/2 t finely grated lime peel
      Add enough milk (about 1 t) to make
        of spreading consistency

Cut into 28 bars.

(Continued Next Page)

RAISIN BARS (CONTINUED)

Calories per serving: 54

Carbohydrates:	12 g	Fiber:	.4 g
Protein:	1 g	Sodium:	24 mg
		Cholesterol:	0 mg

Total Fat: < 1 g
Saturated Fat: .1 g
Monounsaturated Fat: .1 g

Calories from protein: 6%
Calories from carbohydrates: 89%
Calories from fats: 4%

Raspberry Freeze

In blender or food processor place:
- 1 (10 oz.) pkg. frozen red raspberries
- 2 c buttermilk
- 1 t grated orange peel
- 1 t vanilla

Cover; blend until fluffy. Turn into 9 x 9 x 2 inch pan. Freeze until firm. Break up mixture with a fork; place in bowl. Beat with electric mixer until fluffy. Return to pan. Cover; freeze at least 2 hours.

Remove from freezer and let stand for 30 minutes. Scoop into bowl and combine with:
- 1 c lite Cool Whip

Mix with electric mixer until well-blended. Scoop into dishes. Serves 8.

Calories per serving: 76

Carbohydrates:	13 g	Fiber:	1.6 g
Protein:	2 g	Sodium:	66 mg
		Cholesterol:	2 mg
Total Fat:	2 g		
Saturated Fat:	1 g		
Monounsaturated Fat:	.2 g		

Calories from protein: 12%
Calories from carbohydrates: 68%
Calories from fats: 20%

STRAWBERRY ANGEL SQUARES

Bake and cool as directed on box:
    1 pkg. white angel food cake mix

Cut cake into halves. Freeze one half for future use. Cut other half into 1 inch cubes. Set aside.

In large bowl mix:
    1 c boiling water
    1 pkg. (3 oz.) strawberry flavored gelatin

Stir until gelatin is dissolved, then add:
    1/2 c. pineapple juice (from canned pineapple)

In blender place:
    1 c (1 %) cottage cheese

Blend until smooth. Add gelatin mixture. Cover and blend on medium speed until smooth, about 15 seconds. Return mixture to large bowl. Stir in:
    1 can (15 1/4 oz.) crushed pineapple (no sugar added), drained
    1 c sliced strawberries
    Cake cubes

Pour into a square 8 x 8 x 2 inch baking dish. Refrigerate until firm (at least 6 hours). Garnish with fresh strawberries. Serves 12.

(Continued Next Page)

STRAWBERRY ANGEL SQUARES
(CONTINUED)

Calories per serving: 109

Carbohydrates: 23 g　　Fiber: .7 g
Protein: 4 g　　Sodium: 215 mg
Cholesterol: < 1 mg
Total Fat: < 1 g
Saturated Fat: .1 g
Monounsaturated Fat: .1 g

Calories from protein: 15%
Calories from carbohydrates: 82%
Calories from fats: 3%

DIPS, DRESSINGS & SAUCES

Cheddar Cheese Spread

In blender place:
- 1 c nonfat cheddar cheese, grated
- 1 pkg. (3 oz.) nonfat cream cheese, softened
- 1/2 c skim milk
- 1 T Worcestershire sauce
- 1 t dried chives
- 1/2 t dry mustard
- 1/4 t celery seed
- 1/4 t salt
- 1/4 t dried dill weed

Mix until creamy. Pack into non-metal container. Cover and refrigerate for at least 24 hours. Makes 2 cups. Serving size = 1 tablespoon.

Calories per serving: 24

Carbohydrates: <1 g   Fiber: 0 g
Protein: 3 g   Sodium: 57 mg
Cholesterol: 4 mg
Total Fat: 1 g
Saturated Fat: .8 g
Monounsaturated Fat: .4 g

Calories from protein: 44%
Calories from carbohydrates: 8%
Calories from fats: 48%

CUCUMBER-MUSTARD DIP

In food processor place:
> 1 med. cucumber, pared, halved, seeded and coarsely chopped

Whirl until finely chopped. Add:
> 1/4 c nonfat plain yogurt

Whirl until blended. Turn out into bowl. Add:
> 1/4 c nonfat plain yogurt
> 1/2 c nonfat Miracle Whip
> 1 T spicy mustard
> 1 t dill weed
> 1 1/2 t lemon juice
> 1/4 t pepper
> 1 t sugar

Mix until well-blended. Chill thoroughly. Serve with fresh vegetables. Makes 1 3/4 cups. Serving size = 1 tablespoon.

Calories per serving: 7

Carbohydrates: 1 g	Fiber: .1 g
Protein: 0 g	Sodium: 16 mg
	Cholesterol: 0 mg
Total Fat: 0 g	
Saturated Fat: 0 g	
Monounsaturated Fat: .1 g	

Calories from protein: 17%
Calories from carbohydrates: 52%
Calories from fats: 31%

SPINACH DIP

In food processor place:
- 1 c finely chopped spinach
- 1 c (1%) cottage cheese
- 1/2 c nonfat sour cream
- 1/4 c chopped scallions
- 1 t lemon juice
- 1 t oregano
- 1/4 t garlic powder
- 1/2 t cilantro leaves
- 1/2 t salt-free seasoning
- 1/4 c skim milk

Process until well-blended. Cover and refrigerate for at least 4 hours before serving. Makes 3 cups. Serve with raw vegetables. Serving size = 2 tablespoons.

Calories per serving: 14

Carbohydrates: 4 g Fiber: .1 g
Protein: 1 g Sodium: 44 mg
Cholesterol: < 1 mg
Total Fat: < 1 g
Saturated Fat: .5 g
Monounsaturated Fat: 0 g

Calories from protein: 40%
Calories from carbohydrates: 22%
Calories from fats: 38%

VEGETABLE DIP

In food processor place:
    1 c (1 %) lowfat cottage cheese
    1/2 c plain nonfat yogurt

Blend until smooth, then add:
    1/2 t dill weed
    1 clove garlic, minced
    2 green onions, chopped
    1 T fresh parsley, chopped

Mix well, then pour into bowl. Cover and chill. Makes 1 1/2 cups. Serving size = 1/4 cup.

Calories per serving: 40

Carbohydrates:	3 g	Fiber:	.2 g
Protein:	6 g	Sodium:	168 mg
		Cholesterol:	2 mg
Total Fat:	< 1 g		
Saturated Fat:	.2 g		
Monounsaturated Fat:	.1 g		

Calories from protein: 60%
Calories from carbohydrates: 30%
Calories from fats: 10%

BLEU CHEESE DRESSING

Place in food processor or blender:
        1/2 c crumbled bleu cheese
        1/2 c nonfat plain yogurt
        1/2 c nonfat cottage cheese
        1 clove garlic, finely chopped
        1/4 t dry mustard
        1/8 t pepper
        3 T skim milk

Blend until smooth. Add more milk, if necessary. Makes 1 1/2 cups. Serving size = 2 tablespoons.

Calories per serving: 48

    Carbohydrates: 1.5 g   Fiber: 0 g
           Protein: 4 g   Sodium: 182 mg
                             Cholesterol: 8 mg
    Total Fat: 3 g
                  Saturated Fat: 1.9 g
          Monounsaturated Fat: .8 g

          Calories from protein: 33%
    Calories from carbohydrates: 13%
              Calories from fats: 54%

CREAMY DRESSING

In food processor or blender place:
- 1 3/4 c (1 %) cottage cheese
- 4 T vinegar
- 4 t chopped chives
- 2 t grated onions
- 3 dashes Tabasco

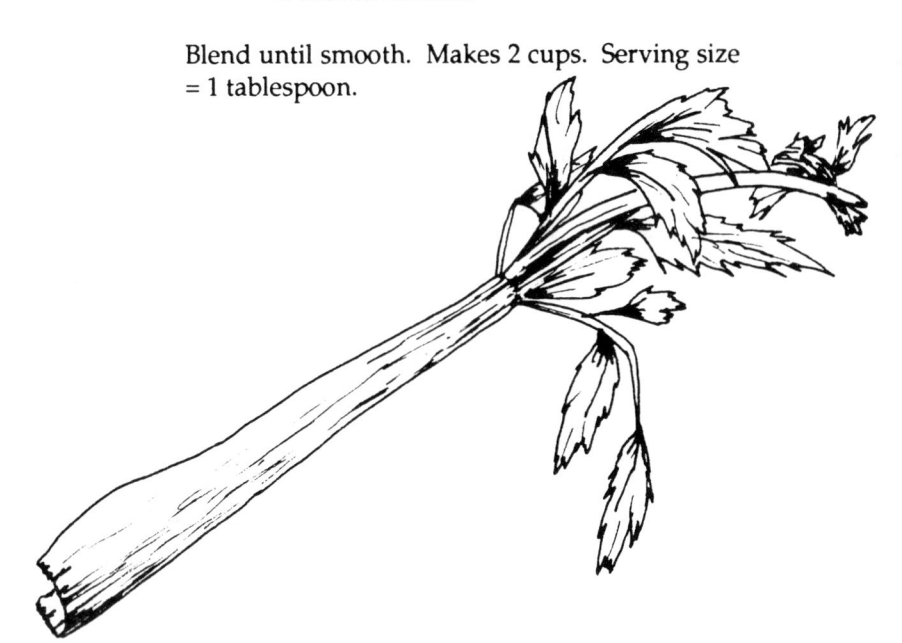

Blend until smooth. Makes 2 cups. Serving size = 1 tablespoon.

Calories per serving: 9

Carbohydrates:	< 1 g	Fiber:	0 g
Protein:	2 g	Sodium:	50 mg
		Cholesterol:	< 1 mg
Total Fat:	0 g		
Saturated Fat:	0 g		
Monounsaturated Fat:	0 g		

Calories from protein: 67%
Calories from carbohydrates: 20%
Calories from fats: 12%

CREAMY GARLIC DRESSING

In bowl combine:
- 1/2 c buttermilk
- 1/2 c plain nonfat yogurt
- 1 T nonfat Miracle Whip
- 1 clove garlic, minced
- 1 t Dijon mustard
- 1/4 t pepper
- 1/2 t sugar

Refrigerate, covered. Makes 1 1/4 cups. Serving size = 1 tablespoon.

Calories per serving: 8

Carbohydrates: 1 g Fiber: 0 g
Protein: < 1 g Sodium: 18 mg
Cholesterol: < 1 mg
Total Fat: < 1 g
Saturated Fat: .1 g
Monounsaturated Fat: .1 g

Calories from protein: 27%
Calories from carbohydrates: 50%
Calories from fats: 24%

LEMON BASIL SALAD DRESSING

In shaker container add:
- 1/3 c lemon juice
- 1 1/2 t dry mustard
- 1 t sugar
- 1 t lite olive oil
- 1/4 t salt
- 1/4 t garlic powder
- 1/4 t pepper
- 1/2 c rice vinegar
- 1/2 t basil

Store in refrigerator, covered. Serve over greens or raw vegetables. Serves 16.

Calories per serving: 6

Carbohydrates:	1 g	Fiber:	0 g
Protein:	0 g	Sodium:	34 mg
		Cholesterol:	0 mg
Total Fat:	< 1 g		
Saturated Fat:	0 g		
Monounsaturated Fat:	.2 g		

Calories from protein: 2 %
Calories from carbohydrates: 63%
Calories from fats: 36%

ORANGE DRESSING

In blender combine:
- 1/2 c orange juice (unsweetened), diluted
- 1 T lemon juice
- 1 t grated orange rind
- 1 t Dijon mustard
- 2 T chopped parsley
- 1 T red wine vinegar

Blend until smooth. Chill for 1 hour. Makes 3/4 cup.

Serve over fruit salad, spinach salad or tossed green salad. Serving size = 1 tablespoon.

Calories per serving: 20

Carbohydrates: 5 g	Fiber: .2 g
Protein: 0 g	Sodium: 6 mg
	Cholesterol: 0 mg
Total Fat: 0 g	
Saturated Fat: 0 g	
Monounsaturated Fat: 0 g	

Calories from protein: 6%
Calories from carbohydrates: 92%
Calories from fats: 2%

SALAD DRESSING

In blender place:
- 1/2 c nonfat plain yogurt
- 1/2 c (1%) lowfat cottage cheese
- 1/8 t garlic powder
- 1/2 t dill weed
- 1/2 t caraway seeds
- 1 T wine vinegar
- 1 t onion flakes
- 1/2 packet artificial sweetener
- 2 T skim milk

Mix well. Add more skim milk, if needed. Refrigerate. Makes 1 cup. Serving size = 1 tablespoon.

Calories per serving: 10

Carbohydrates:	1g	Fiber:	0g
Protein:	1g	Sodium:	35 mg
		Cholesterol:	0 mg
Total Fat:	0g		
Saturated Fat:	0g		
Monounsaturated Fat:	0g		

Calories from protein: 53%
Calories from carbohydrates: 38%
Calories from fats: 9%

BLUEBERRY SAUCE

Slightly thaw:
    2 c frozen unsweetened blueberries

Set 1 cup aside. Place remaining 1 cup in small saucepan. Add:
    1 T honey
    1 t grated lemon peel
    1/2 t cinnamon

Cook mixture 4 to 5 minutes over medium heat, stirring and crushing berries.

In small bowl stir:
    2 T cold water
    1 t cornstarch

Add mixture to saucepan. Cook 1 to 2 minutes longer. Add remaining berries. Cook for 1 to 2 more minutes. Remove from heat. Stir in:
    1 T diet margarine

Serve warm. Makes 1 1/4 cups. Serving size = 2 tablespoons.

Calories per serving: 28

    Carbohydrates: 6 g   Fiber: 1 g
         Protein: 0 g   Sodium: 14 mg
                            Cholesterol: 0 mg
      Total Fat: < 1 g
          Saturated Fat: 0 g
    Monounsaturated Fat: 0 g

        Calories from protein: 2%
  Calories from carbohydrates: 76%
          Calories from fats: 22%

Marinara Sauce

In skillet sauté:
- 1 med. onion, chopped
- 1 t olive oil

Cook for 4 to 5 minutes, then add:
- 4 cloves garlic, crushed
- 1 (28 oz.) can crushed tomatoes (low-salt)
- 1 (16 oz.) can tomato sauce (low-salt)
- 2 c broccoli, chopped
- 2 c cauliflower, chopped
- 2 carrots, sliced
- 1 T dried parsley
- 2 t basil
- 2 t oregano

Bring to a boil. Lower heat, cover and simmer 30 minutes. Makes 6 cups. Serving size = 1/2 cup.

Calories per serving: 58

Carbohydrates:	12 g	Fiber:	4 g
Protein:	3 g	Sodium:	32 mg
		Cholesterol:	0 mg
Total Fat:	< 1 g		
Saturated Fat:	.1 g		
Monounsaturated Fat:	.3 g		

Calories from protein: 17%
Calories from carbohydrates: 72%
Calories from fats: 11%

Mexican Sauce

In saucepan combine:
- 1 can (8 oz.) tomato sauce (no salt added)
- 1/4 t garlic powder
- 1/2 t cumin
- 1/8 t cayenne powder
- 1 t jalapeno peppers
- 1 T lemon juice
- 1 T sugar

Cook until thoroughly heated. Makes 1 1/4 cups. Serve over rice or burritos. Serving size = 1/4 cup.

Calories per serving: 26

Carbohydrates:	6 g	Fiber:	.7 g
Protein:	0 g	Sodium:	13 mg
		Cholesterol:	0 mg
Total Fat:	0 g		
Saturated Fat:	0 g		
Monounsaturated Fat:	0 g		

Calories from protein: 9%
Calories from carbohydrates: 86%
Calories from fats: 4%

Papaya Marinade

In bowl combine:
    2 c dry sherry
    Juice of 1 fresh lime
    2 T soy sauce
    1/2 c fresh or canned papaya, mashed
    2 T brown sugar
    1 t minced fresh ginger
    1 clove garlic, crushed
    1/2 t salt

Makes approximately 3 cups. Use for chicken, turkey or pork. Serving size = 2 tablespoons.

Calories per serving: 31

Carbohydrates: 2g
Protein: 0g
Fiber: .1 g
Sodium: 133 mg
Cholesterol: 0 mg
Total Fat: 0g
Saturated Fat: 0g
Monounsaturated Fat: 0g

Calories from protein: 2%
Calories from carbohydrates: 26%
Calories from fat: 0%
Other Calories (i.e. alcohol): 71%

EXTRAS

BUTTER – EXTENDED

In bowl combine:
    1 c butter
    1/3 c canola oil

Dissolve 1 package gelatin in 1 cup water.

Add to butter mixture.

Whip with electric blender. Add 1/2 cup water and whip until fluffy. Makes 3 cups. Serving size = 1 Tablespoon.

Calories per serving: 16

Carbohydrates:	0g	Fiber:	0g
Protein:	0g	Sodium:	11 mg
		Cholesterol:	3 mg
Total Fat:	2g		
Saturated Fat:	.8 g		
Monounsaturated Fat:	.7 g		

Calories from protein: 1%
Calories from carbohydrates: 0%
Calories from fats: 99%

CINNAMON APPLE OATMEAL

Place in pan:
    1 c water
    3/4 c apple juice, undiluted
    2 T raisins
    1/2 t cinnamon

Bring to boil, then stir in:
    3/4 c quick cooking oats
    2 1/2 T dry evaporated milk

Stir for 2 minutes. Remove from heat and stir in:
    2/3 c chopped apple
    1 1/2 t brown sugar

Stir slightly. Let set for 5 minutes. Serves 2.

Calories per serving: 245

Carbohydrates:	52 g	Fiber:	4.3 g
Protein:	7 g	Sodium:	36 mg
		Cholesterol:	1 mg
Total Fat:	2 g		
Saturated Fat:	.4 g		
Monounsaturated Fat:	.7 g		

Calories from protein: 11%
Calories from carbohydrates: 81%
Calories from fats: 8%

Fresh Salsa

In medium bowl combine:
- 2 c chopped tomato
- 1/2 c chopped green onion
- 1/4 c chopped green pepper
- 2 T fresh parsley
- 1 T lemon juice
- 1 c low-sodium tomato sauce
- 1/4 t black pepper
- 3 t green chilies

Mix well and chill. Makes 4 cups.

Calories per serving: 40

Carbohydrates: 9 g Fiber: 3 g
Protein: 2 g Sodium: 15 mg
Cholesterol: 0 mg
Total Fat: 0 g
Saturated Fat: 0 g
Monounsaturated Fat: .2 g

Calories from protein: 16%
Calories from carbohydrates: 76%
Calories from fats: 8%

Ginger Pancakes

In bowl place:
- 2 1/2 c unbleached flour
- 1 T plus 2 t baking powder
- 1/2 t salt
- 1 t baking soda
- 1/2 t ginger
- 1/4 c molasses
- 2 c skim milk
- 3 egg whites
- 1/4 c diet margarine
- 2 T apple juice, undiluted

Beat with electric mixer until blended. Fold in:
- 1 c raisins

Drop batter by 1/4 cup onto lightly greased griddle. Cook until bubbles form on surface of pancake. Turn and cook until brown on bottom. Makes 22 pancakes.

Calories per serving: 103

Carbohydrates:	20 g	Fiber:	1 g
Protein:	3 g	Sodium:	205 mg
		Cholesterol:	0 mg
Total Fat:	1 g		
Saturated Fat:	.3 g		
Monounsaturated Fat:	.4 g		

Calories from protein: 11%
Calories from carbohydrates: 78%
Calories from fats: 11%

GLAZED APPLES

Core and slice into 1 inch rings:
    3 lg. apples

In skillet sprayed with vegetable spray place:
    1 T diet margarine
    1 T apple juice, undiluted

Heat until melted, then add:
    2 T brown sugar
    3/4 t cinnamon

When sugar dissolves, add apple rings. Cook, turning gently for 7 to 10 minutes or until fruit is tender. Serves 4.

Calories per serving: 140

    Carbohydrates: 33 g   Fiber: 4.5 g
    Protein: < 1 g   Sodium: 40 mg
    Cholesterol: 0 mg
    Total Fat: 2 g
    Saturated Fat: .4 g
    Monounsaturated Fat: .6 g

    Calories from protein: 1%
    Calories from carbohydrates: 87%
    Calories from fats: 12%

Goulash

In skillet sprayed with vegetable spray brown:
    1/2 lb. buffalo meat
    1/2 c chopped onion
    1/2 t garlic powder

Add:
    1/2 c chopped celery leaves
    1 med. tomato, chopped
    1 t oregano
    1 c spaghetti sauce (low-salt, lowfat)
    1 c hot water
    1/2 c cooked kidney beans

Simmer for 20 to 30 minutes. Add:
    3 c cooked Garden Medley rotini noodles

Heat thoroughly. Serves 8.

Calories per serving: 160

Carbohydrates:	20 g	Fiber:	2 g
Protein:	11 g	Sodium:	40 mg
		Cholesterol:	20 mg
Total Fat:	4 g		
Saturated Fat:	1.1 g		
Monounsaturated Fat:	1.8 g		

Calories from protein: 27%
Calories from carbohydrates: 49%
Calories from fats: 24%

HERBED CARROTS

Place in small saucepan:
>3 c carrot sticks

Cover with cold water and cook on medium-high; bring to boil. Reduce heat to medium; cover carrots and cook for 3 minutes. Add:
>1 c pearl onions
>1/4 c dry white wine

Bring to boil and simmer 3 minutes longer. Drain carrots and onions and transfer to serving bowl. In same pot mix:
>2 t diet margarine
>1 t instant chicken granules (salt-free)
>1 t salt-free lemon and herb seasoning
>1 t honey

Simmer for 1 minute. Toss mixture with carrots and onions. Serves 4.

Calories per serving: 94

Carbohydrates:	17 g	Fiber:	4.7 g
Protein:	2 g	Sodium:	134 mg
		Cholesterol:	< 1 mg
Total Fat:	1 g		
Saturated Fat:	.3 g		
Monounsaturated Fat:	.5 g		

Calories from protein: 9%
Calories from carbohydrates: 77%
Calories from fats: 14%

Parmesan Crisps

Cut and make 8 rounds:
    4 (4 in.) whole wheat pitas

In saucepan place:
    2 T diet margarine
    1 sm. clove garlic, crushed

Stir and heat until margarine is melted. Remove from heat; brush mixture over inside surface of each pita round.

In small bowl combine:
    2 T freshly grated Parmesan cheese
    1/4 t oregano
    1/8 t paprika

Sprinkle evenly over pita rounds. Cut each round into quarters; place each on ungreased cookie sheets. Bake at 375° for 15 minutes or until crisp. Makes 32 crisps.

Calories per serving: 25

Carbohydrates:	4 g	Fiber:	.1 g
Protein:	1 g	Sodium:	57 mg
		Cholesterol:	0 mg
Total Fat:	< 1 g		
Saturated Fat:	.1 g		
Monounsaturated Fat:	.2 g		

Calories from protein: 15%
Calories from carbohydrates: 66%
Calories from fats: 20%

Pizza Roll

Thaw and let rise slightly:
    1 loaf frozen bread dough

Roll dough out on floured surface until it forms into a rectangle, about 10 x 17 inch.

With the bottom or a spoon spread:
    1/3 c barbecue sauce

Top with:
    1 can (10 oz.) white chicken
      (water packed)

Slice thin and separate rings of:
    1/2 red onion

Arrange onion slices on top of chicken. Then top with:
    1 tomato, finely chopped

Sprinkle with:
    1/3 c grated mozzarella cheese
    1 T parsley flakes

Roll, from the long side. Place roll on cookie sheet sprayed with vegetable spray in a U-shape. Bake at 350° for 30 to 35 minutes. Serves 8.

(Continued Next Page)

Pizza Roll (Continued)

Calories per serving: 267

Carbohydrates: 33 g Fiber: 3.5 g
Protein: 22 g Sodium: 503 mg
Cholesterol: 36 mg
Total Fat: 6 g
Saturated Fat: 2 g
Monounsaturated Fat: 2 g

Calories from protein: 32%
Calories from carbohydrates: 48%
Calories from fats: 20%

SPICY TOMATO SAUCE

In bowl combine:
- 1/2 c ketchup
- 4 t Worcestershire sauce
- 2 t vinegar
- 1 1/2 T chopped chives
- 1/4 t pepper

Makes 3/4 cup.

Great on potatoes, rice, pasta, poultry, etc. Serving size = 1/4 cup.

Calories per serving: 52

Carbohydrates:	12 g	Fiber:	.3 g
Protein:	1 g	Sodium:	603 mg
		Cholesterol:	0 mg
Total Fat:	< 1 g		
Saturated Fat:	0 g		
Monounsaturated Fat:	0 g		

Calories from protein: 9%
Calories from carbohydrates: 88%
Calories from fats: 3%

STUFFED RED PEPPERS

Cut off tops, wash and remove seeds from:
    4 red peppers

In bowl combine:
    2 c (1%) cottage cheese
    1/4 t pepper
    2 T chopped chives
    2 T grated carrots
    2 T chopped celery
    1/2 t salt-free seasoning

Spoon mixture into peppers. Sprinkle with paprika. Chill. Serves 4.

Calories per serving: 103

Carbohydrates: 8 g   Fiber: 1.3 g
    Protein: 15 g   Sodium: 466 mg
                     Cholesterol: 5 mg
Total Fat: 2 g
    Saturated Fat: .8 g
    Monounsaturated Fat: .4 g

Calories from protein: 57%
Calories from carbohydrates: 30%
Calories from fats: 13%

TANGY FRENCH TOAST

Arrange in 13 x 9 inch baking dish:
    1 loaf French bread, cut into 1 in. thick slices (10 to 12 slices)

In bowl combine:
    1 1/2 c skim milk
    5 egg whites
    2 T brown sugar
    1/4 c orange juice, diluted
    1 T orange extract
    1 T vanilla extract

Beat with fork until well-blended. Pour over bread slices. Cover and refrigerate at least 1 hour. (Can keep longer.)

Transfer bread slices to cookie sheet sprayed with vegetable spray. Make sure that slices don't touch. Bake at 400° for 20 to 25 minutes, until puffed and lightly browned. Turn bread slices a few times to keep from burning on either side. Serves 6.

Calories per serving: 257

Carbohydrates: 44 g   Fiber: 1.3 g
Protein: 12 g   Sodium: 481 mg
Cholesterol: 1 mg
Total Fat: 3 g
Saturated Fat: .7 g
Monounsaturated Fat: .9 g

Calories from protein: 19%
Calories from carbohydrates: 71%
Calories from fats: 10%

VEGETABLE CASSEROLE

In skillet sprayed with vegetable spray sauté:
- 1 T diet margarine
- 1 c thinly sliced onions
- 1 clove garlic, minced

Sauté for 5 minutes; add:
- 1 c zucchini, thinly sliced
- 2 c green beans (canned or frozen)
- 1 1/2 c corn (frozen)
- 1 c chopped tomatoes
- 1 c chopped carrots
- 1/2 t salt
- 1/2 t pepper
- 1 t lemon juice
- 1/2 c water

Cook for 5 minutes. Spoon into casserole dish sprayed with vegetable spray. Cover and bake at 350° for 40 to 45 minutes, stirring occasionally. Add more water during cooking, if necessary. Serves 10.

Calories per serving: 48

Carbohydrates:	10 g	Fiber:	3 g
Protein:	2 g	Sodium:	131 mg
		Cholesterol:	0 mg
Total Fat:	< 1 g		
Saturated Fat:	.1 g		
Monounsaturated Fat:	.2 g		

Calories from protein: 12%
Calories from carbohydrates: 76%
Calories from fats: 12%

Vegetable Pizza

In large bowl combine:
- 2 1/2 c unbleached flour
- 1 pkg. fast-rising dry yeast
- 1/2 t salt

Add:
- 1 c very hot water
- 1 T olive oil

Turn dough onto floured surface; cover with bowl. Let rise 10 minutes.

Roll dough into a 14 inch round; place on baking sheet sprayed with vegetable spray.

In saucepan combine:
- 1 can (15 oz.) chopped tomatoes
- 1 can (6 oz.) tomato paste (no salt added)
- 1 med. onion, chopped
- 1 T basil
- 1 T oregano
- 1 T parsley
- 1/4 t garlic powder
- 1/4 t pepper

Bring to boil; simmer 10 to 15 minutes.

Spread pizza sauce on dough. Sprinkle with:
- 1/4 c green pepper, chopped
- 1/4 c mushrooms, chopped
- 1/4 c fresh spinach, chopped
- 1/2 c lowfat mozzarella cheese

Bake at 450° for 10 to 15 minutes or until crust is done and cheese is melted. Serves 6.

(Continued Next Page)

VEGETABLE PIZZA (CONTINUED)

Calories per serving: 293

Carbohydrates: 52 g   Fiber: 4.3 g
Protein: 11 g   Sodium: 246 mg
Cholesterol: 5 mg
Total Fat: 5 g
Saturated Fat: 1.5 g
Monounsaturated Fat: 2.2 g

Calories from protein: 15%
Calories from carbohydrates: 70%
Calories from fats: 15%

ZUCCHINI TOMATO BAKE

In skillet sprayed with vegetable spray place:
    1 T diet margarine
    1 c onion, sliced
    2 med. zucchini, sliced

Sauté until crisp-tender. Add:
    1 t basil

Spoon mixture into 2 quart baking dish sprayed with vegetable spray. Top with:
    2 c (1%) cottage cheese

Arrange on top:
    2 med. tomatoes, sliced

Sprinkle with:
    1/2 c bread crumbs

Bake at 350° for 20 to 30 minutes. Serves 6.

Calories per serving: 118

    Carbohydrates: 13 g   Fiber: 2.2 g
    Protein: 11 g   Sodium: 395 mg
    Cholesterol: 4 mg
    Total Fat: 2 g
    Saturated Fat: .8 g
    Monounsaturated Fat: .7 g

    Calories from protein: 38%
    Calories from carbohydrates: 45%
    Calories from fats: 17%

HOT CRANBERRY SIPPER

Combine in large saucepan:
- 2 c cranberry juice (unsweetened)
- 1 (6 oz.) can unsweetened pineapple juice
- 1/2 c orange juice (unsweetened), diluted
- 1/4 c lemon juice
- 1/2 c red currant jelly
- 1/4 t allspice

Cook over medium heat until jelly melts and mixture is thoroughly heated, stirring well. Serve hot. Makes 1 quart. Serving size = 1/2 cup.

Calories per serving: 228

Carbohydrates:	58 g	Fiber:	.9 g
Protein:	<1 g	Sodium:	10 mg
		Cholesterol:	0 mg
Total Fat:	<1 g		
Saturated Fat:	0 g		
Monounsaturated Fat:	0 g		

Calories from protein: 1%
Calories from carbohydrates: 98%
Calories from fat: 1%

MARMALADE TEA

Steep for 5 minutes:
    1 family size tea bag
    5 c boiling water

Remove tea bag. Stir in:
    1/2 c orange marmalade
    2 T sugar
    2 T lemon juice

Strain mixture, if desired. Serve hot. Serves 6.

Calories per serving: 88

    Carbohydrates: 24 g   Fiber: .2 g
    Protein: 0 g   Sodium: 11 mg
        Cholesterol: 0 mg
    Total Fat: 0 g
    Saturated Fat: 0 g
    Monounsaturated Fat: 0 g

    Calories from protein: 0%
    Calories from carbohydrates: 99%
    Calories from fats: 0%

ORANGE WASSAIL

In large pot add:
- 1 (64 oz.) carton orange juice (unsweetened)
- 1 (64 oz.) jar apple juice (unsweetened)
- 1 (32 oz.) jar cranberry juice
- 1 (12 oz.) can frozen lemonade, thawed and undiluted
- 1 stick cinnamon

Cook over medium heat 5 to 10 minutes.

Insert 1 tablespoon whole cloves into 2 oranges, sectioned.

Add to mixture. Cook thoroughly. Serve hot. Makes 5 1/2 quarts. Serving size = 1/2 cup.

Calories per serving: 277

Carbohydrates:	69 g	Fiber:	2 g
Protein:	2 g	Sodium:	9 mg
		Cholesterol:	0 mg
Total Fat:	< 1 g		
Saturated Fat:	.1 g		
Monounsaturated Fat:	.1 g		

Calories from protein: 2%
Calories from carbohydrates: 96%
Calories from fats: 1%

PUNCH

Pour into large punch bowl:
    1 (46 oz.) can unsweetened pineapple juice
    2 (6 oz.) cans frozen lemonade
    8 c water
    1 (2 liter) ginger ale

Slice and add to punch as garnish:
    1 lemon
    1 orange

Serves 31. Serving size = 6 ounces.

Calories per serving: 68

Carbohydrates:	17 g	Fiber:	.3 g
Protein:	0 g	Sodium:	5 mg
		Cholesterol:	0 mg
Total Fat:	0 g		
Saturated Fat:	0 g		
Monounsaturated Fat:	0 g		

Calories from protein: 1%
Calories from carbohydrates: 98%
Calories from fats: 1%

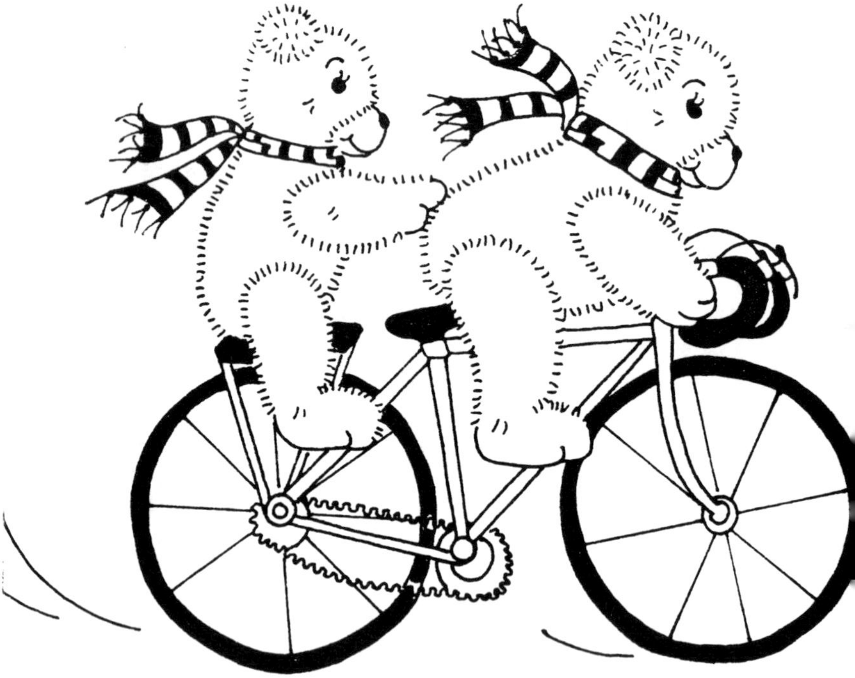

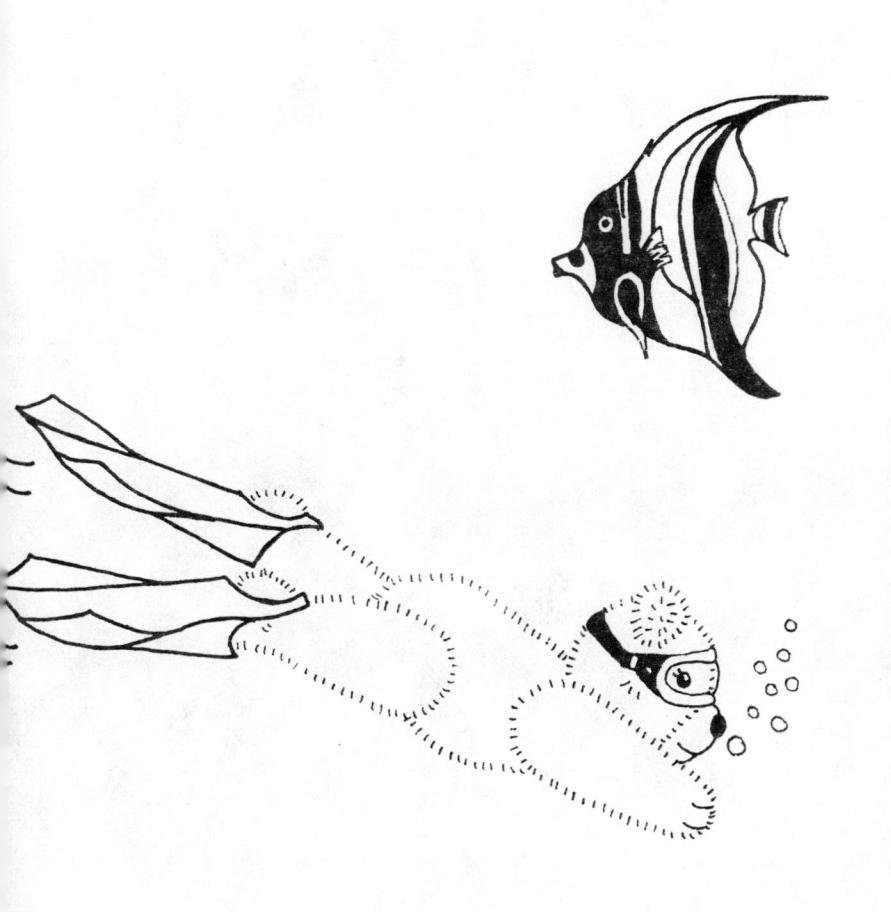

FISH & POULTRY

EASY HALIBUT

In 8 inch square pan place:
- 4 (4 oz.) halibut steaks
- 1 1/2 c finely chopped Golden Delicious apples

In small bowl mix:
- 1/4 c raspberry juice, diluted
- 1 T brandy
- 1 T diet margarine, melted
- 1/4 t salt
- 1/4 t pepper

Pour mixture over fish and apples. Sprinkle with:
- 1 T chopped chives

Bake, uncovered, at 350° for 20 to 25 minutes or until fish flakes. Serves 4.

Calories per serving: 208

Carbohydrates:	17 g	Fiber:	3 g
Protein:	22 g	Sodium:	242 mg
		Cholesterol:	57 mg
Total Fat:	4 g		
Saturated Fat:	1 g		
Monounsaturated Fat:	1 g		

Calories from protein: 42%
Calories from carbohydrates: 33%
Calories from fats: 17%
Other Calories (i.e. alcohol): 8%

GRILLED SHARK

In small bowl combine:
>3 T soy sauce (low-salt)
>2 T lemon juice
>1/4 t ginger
>1/4 t dry mustard
>1 T cooking wine

Rinse:
>1 lb. shark steaks

Brush sauce mixture on steaks and marinate for 1 hour.

Grill steaks until thoroughly cooked. Serves 4.

Calories per serving: 106

Carbohydrates:	1 g	Fiber:	0 g
Protein:	22 g	Sodium:	281 mg
		Cholesterol:	51 mg
Total Fat:	1 g		
Saturated Fat:	.5 g		
Monounsaturated Fat:	.5 g		

Calories from protein: 86%
Calories from carbohydrates: 5%
Calories from fats: 9%

HALIBUT

Place in casserole dish sprayed with vegetable spray:
>1 lb. halibut

Place on top:
>1/2 c chopped onion
>1/2 c chopped red pepper
>1/2 c chopped green pepper

In small bowl combine:
>1 T white wine
>1 T Worcestershire sauce
>1 t basil
>1/4 t dill weed
>1/2 t garlic salt

Pour over fish. Bake at 350° for 10 minutes. Sprinkle with:
>1 T fresh grated Parmesan cheese

Bake for 5 to 10 more minutes, until fish flakes. Serves 6.

Calories per serving: 91

Carbohydrates:	2 g	Fiber:	.6 g
Protein:	14 g	Sodium:	283 mg
		Cholesterol:	42 mg
Total Fat:	2.5 g		
Saturated Fat:	.5 g		
Monounsaturated Fat:	.8 g		

Calories from protein: 64%
Calories from carbohydrates: 11%
Calories from fats: 25%

SALMON LOAF

In milk, soak 3 slices of bread until bread is saturated. Place in bowl and tear into small pieces.

Drain and clean:
    1 can (15 1/2 oz.) cooked salmon

Add to bread mixture. In small bowl beat:
    1 egg white

Add to bread mixture, then add:
    2 T parsley
    1 T minced onion
    1/2 t dill weed
    1/4 c skim milk

Spray with vegetable spray a 7 1/2 x 4 inch loaf pan. Place mixture into pan. Bake at 350° for 30 minutes. Serves 6.

Calories per serving: 151

    Carbohydrates: 8 g   Fiber: .6 g
    Protein: 17 g   Sodium: 460 mg
                         Cholesterol: 30 mg
    Total Fat: 5 g
        Saturated Fat: .9 g
        Monounsaturated Fat: 1.4 g

    Calories from protein: 48%
    Calories from carbohydrates: 22%
    Calories from fats: 30%

Salmon Pasta

In bowl combine:
- 1 c grated carrots
- 1 can (6 1/2 oz.) salmon (water packed)
- 1/4 c chopped green pepper
- 1/4 c chopped red onion
- 1 T parsley
- 1 t salt-free Original Seasoning

Add:
- 3 c cooked macaroni noodles

Toss with:
- 5 T Dorothy Lynch lowfat salad dressing

Refrigerate for 1 hour before serving. Serves 6.

Calories per serving: 125

Carbohydrates:	15 g	Fiber:	1 g
Protein:	8 g	Sodium:	266 mg
		Cholesterol:	13 mg
Total Fat:	3 g		
Saturated Fat:	.4 g		
Monounsaturated Fat:	.8 g		

Calories from protein: 28%
Calories from carbohydrates: 52%
Calories from fats: 20%

SALMON STEAKS

Rinse and place on aluminum foil on grill:
    4 (4 oz.) salmon steaks

Sprinkle with:
    1 T coarsely ground black pepper
    1 T lemon juice
    1 t thyme

Top with:
    1/2 med. onion, very thinly sliced

Grill for 10 to 15 minutes, until flaky. Serves 4.

Calories per serving: 149

Carbohydrates:	2 g	Fiber:	.4 g
Protein:	21 g	Sodium:	56 mg
		Cholesterol:	60 mg
Total Fat:	5 g		
Saturated Fat:	1 g		
Monounsaturated Fat:	2 g		

Calories from protein: 61%
Calories from carbohydrates: 6%
Calories from fats: 33%

Tuna Potato Dish

Spray 8 1/2 x 11 inch casserole dish with vegetable spray.

In microwave cook for 10 to 15 minutes:
>3 med. potatoes

Slice potatoes into thin slices. Arrange potatoes in casserole dish. Top with:
>1/4 c skim milk
>1 T parsley flakes
>1/4 c grated lowfat cheddar

In small bowl toss:
>1 (6 1/8 oz.) white tuna (water packed)
>1/4 c chopped celery leaves
>1 T minced onion
>1 med. carrot, grated

Spread tuna mixture over potato mixture evenly. On top, crumble:
>1/2 c lowfat ricotta cheese

Sprinkle on top:
>1/3 c lowfat mozzarella cheese, grated
>1/4 c skim milk
>1 T Parmesan cheese

Cover and bake at 400° for 20 minutes. Remove cover and bake for an additional 5 to 10 minutes. Serves 8.

(Continued Next Page)

TUNA POTATO DISH (CONTINUED)

Calories per serving: 199

Carbohydrates: 22 g Fiber: 2 g
Protein: 17 g Sodium: 266 mg
Cholesterol: 27 mg
Total Fat: 5 g
Saturated Fat: 3 g
Monounsaturated Fat: 1.3 g

Calories from protein: 35%
Calories from carbohydrates: 44%
Calories from fats: 22%

TUNA STIR-FRY

In skillet place:
- 2 T oil-free Italian dressing
- 1/2 c chopped onion
- 1 lg. clove garlic, minced
- 1 c carrots, sliced thinly
- 1 c celery, sliced thinly
- 1/2 c green pepper, chopped
- 1/2 c red pepper, chopped
- 1/2 c broccoli, chopped

Cook on medium-high for about 5 minutes. Add:
- 2 cans (6 1/8 oz.) white tuna (water packed)
- 3 T soy sauce
- 1 T lemon juice
- 1 T parsley
- 2 T water

Stir and cook until thoroughly heated. Serve over:
- 3 c cooked brown rice

Serves 6.

Calories per serving: 229

Carbohydrates:	32 g	Fiber:	3.5 g
Protein:	21 g	Sodium:	851 mg
		Cholesterol:	27 mg
Total Fat:	2 g		
Saturated Fat:	.4 g		
Monounsaturated Fat:	.4 g		

Calories from protein: 37%
Calories from carbohydrates: 57%
Calories from fats: 6%

TUNA-TOPPED BAGELS

In bowl combine:
- 1 can (6 1/8 oz.) white tuna (water packed)
- 2 T nonfat Miracle Whip
- 2 t mustard
- 1 T parsley
- 1 t Spike seasoning

Slice 3 oat bran bagels in half. Top each half with tuna mixture.

Slice into thin slices and place on top of each half:
- 1 lg. tomato

On top of each tomato slice place:
- 1 thin slice mozzarella cheese (1/2 oz. slice)

Place bagel halves on cookie sheet. Broil in oven until cheese melts and browns slightly. Serves 6.

Calories per serving: 180

Carbohydrates:	19 g	Fiber:	.7 g
Protein:	18 g	Sodium:	404 mg
		Cholesterol:	25 mg
Total Fat:	3 g		
Saturated Fat:	2 g		
Monounsaturated Fat:	1 g		

Calories from protein: 40%
Calories from carbohydrates: 43%
Calories from fats: 18%

Apple-Honey Chicken

In large bowl combine:
- 1/4 t cinnamon
- 2 c unsweetened apple juice, diluted

Add:
- 1 lb. boneless, skinless chicken breasts

Marinate in refrigerator for 1 or more hours. In skillet sprayed with vegetable spray sauté:
- 1 T apple juice
- 1 lg. apple, cored, sliced into thin slices

Turning, cook for 5 minutes. Remove apples from skillet. Remove chicken from marinade, reserving marinade. In plastic bag combine:
- 1/4 c flour
- 1/4 t salt
- 1/2 t ground pepper
- 1/4 t paprika

Place chicken into bag, one at a time. Shake to coat. In skillet place:
- 1 T diet margarine

Place chicken in skillet. Cook over medium heat, turning until both sides are brown, 10 to 15 minutes. Pour 1/2 cup marinade over chicken and drizzle on top:
- 1 T honey

Add:
- 2 c cooked brown rice

Cook for 5 to 10 minutes or until chicken is done. Serves 4.

(Continued Next Page)

APPLE-HONEY CHICKEN (CONTINUED)

Calories per serving: 393

Carbohydrates: 54 g Fiber: 2.7 g
Protein: 30 g Sodium: 237 mg
Cholesterol: 72 mg
Total Fat: 6 g
Saturated Fat: 1.6 g
Monounsaturated Fat: 2 g

Calories from protein: 31%
Calories from carbohydrates: 55%
Calories from fats: 14%

BREADED CHICKEN BREASTS

In small bowl combine:
- 1/4 c seasoned bread crumbs
- 1/4 c grated Parmesan cheese
- 1/2 t oregano
- 1/4 t rosemary
- 1/4 t basil
- 1/4 t pepper

Rinse:
- 4 chicken breasts, skinned and boneless (4 oz. each)

Dip chicken breasts in:
- 1/2 c buttermilk

Roll chicken breasts in bread crumbs/herb mixture. Place chicken breasts in baking pan sprayed with vegetable spray. Bake at 350°, covered, for 20 minutes. Remove cover and continue to bake for 15 to 20 minutes or until done. Serves 4.

Calories per serving: 208
- Carbohydrates: 7 g
- Protein: 30 g
- Fiber: .3 g
- Sodium: 238 mg
- Cholesterol: 77 mg
- Total Fat: 6 g
- Saturated Fat: 2.3 g
- Monounsaturated Fat: 2 g

- Calories from protein: 60%
- Calories from carbohydrates: 13%
- Calories from fats: 27%

Cajun Chicken And Rice

Sauté in pan sprayed with vegetable spray:
   1 lb. chicken breast, cut into strips

Cook until chicken is tender. Then add:
   1 (14 1/2 oz.) can cajun style stewed tomatoes
   1/2 c water
   1 t cilantro leaves
   1/2 t Spike (all-purpose seasoning)
   1/2 c chopped green pepper
   1/4 c chopped onion

Simmer for 30 minutes. Add:
   2 c cooked brown rice

Simmer for 5 more minutes. Serves 6.

Calories per serving: 197

Carbohydrates:	22 g	Fiber:	2.6 g
Protein:	20 g	Sodium:	52 mg
		Cholesterol:	48 mg
Total Fat:	3 g		
Saturated Fat:	.9 g		
Monounsaturated Fat:	1 g		

Calories from protein: 41%
Calories from carbohydrates: 44%
Calories from fats: 15%

Chicken Fajitas

In small bowl combine:
- 2 T lime juice
- 1 T lime juice
- 1 T vinegar
- 1 T Worcestershire sauce
- 1/4 t pepper
- 1/4 t cumin
- 1 T crushed coriander
- 2 cloves garlic, minced

In baking dish place:
- 4 chicken breasts, skinless, boneless, sliced diagonally

Pour marinade over chicken and marinate for at least 4 hours.

Spray skillet with vegetable spray. Then heat for 2 minutes:
- 1 t lite olive oil

Add:
- 1/2 c onion, thinly sliced
- 1/2 c green pepper, thinly sliced
- 1/2 c carrot, thin strips

Place vegetables in skillet and cook for 2 minutes. Remove vegetables; set aside. Place chicken in skillet and cook for 5 minutes or until chicken is tender. Add vegetables to chicken and stir-fry for 2 minutes. Add:
- 1/2 c tomato, chopped

Stir-fry for another 1 to 2 minutes. Serves 6.

Serve on warm tortillas. (Recipe analysis = 1 tortilla.)

(Continued Next Page)

CHICKEN FAJITAS (CONTINUED)

Calories per serving: 230

Carbohydrates: 24 g Fiber: 2 g
Protein: 21 g Sodium: 190 mg
Cholesterol: 48 mg
Total Fat: 6 g
Saturated Fat: 1.2 g
Monounsaturated Fat: 2.6 g

Calories from protein: 36%
Calories from carbohydrates: 41%
Calories from fats: 24%

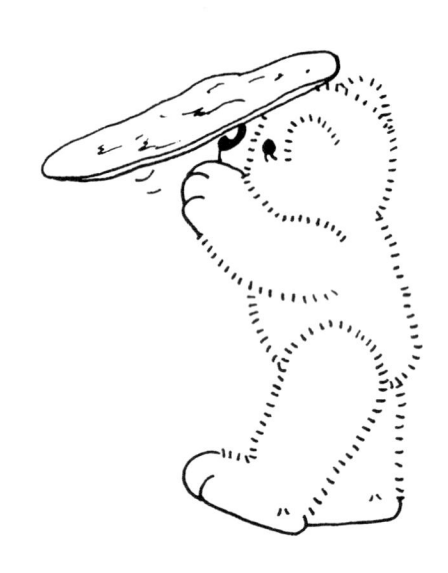

Chicken/Mandarin Salad

In small bowl whisk:
- 4 T nonfat Miracle Whip
- 3 T orange juice, diluted
- 1 t grated orange peel

Whip until smooth and frothy. On small plates arrange spinach leaves (1 cup spinach per plate). In bowl toss lightly:
- 2 cans (5 oz.) white chicken, drained
- 1 c mandarin oranges
- 1/2 c red grapes
- 1/2 c chopped celery
- 2 T sliced almonds

Place chicken mixture on spinach leaves. Drizzle dressing over chicken mixture. Serves 4.

Calories per serving: 237

Carbohydrates: 23 g   Fiber: 4.3 g
Protein: 25 g   Sodium: 135 mg
Cholesterol: 61 mg
Total Fat: 6 g
Saturated Fat: 1.3 g
Monounsaturated Fat: 2.3 g

Calories from protein: 41%
Calories from carbohydrates: 37%
Calories from fats: 22%

Chicken Salad

In small bowl whisk until smooth and frothy:
- 1/4 c nonfat yogurt
- 2 T nonfat Miracle Whip
- 1 T skim milk
- 1/4 t pepper
- 1 t Worcestershire sauce

In large bowl combine:
- 2 c cooked chicken, shredded
- 1/2 c diced celery
- 1/2 c chopped water chestnuts
- 1/2 c grated carrots
- 1 can (7 1/2 oz.) unsweetened crushed pineapple, drained

Toss with dressing. Serve on lettuce leaves. Serves 6.

Calories per serving: 121

Carbohydrates:	9 g	Fiber:	1 g
Protein:	16 g	Sodium:	67 mg
		Cholesterol:	40 mg
Total Fat:	3 g		
Saturated Fat:	.7 g		
Monounsaturated Fat:	.8 g		

Calories from protein: 52%
Calories from carbohydrates: 29%
Calories from fats: 19%

Chicken Stew

In skillet sprayed with vegetable spray sauté:
- 1 lb. chicken breast, cut into cubes
- 1 T diet margarine
- 1 T minced garlic

Cook until browned, about 8 to 10 minutes. Place in crockpot and add:
- 1 (14 1/2 oz.) stewed tomatoes (no salt added)
- 1 (6 oz.) can tomato paste (no salt added)
- 10 pearl onions
- 1 1/2 t ground cumin
- 1 1/2 t salt-free seasoning
- 1 t oregano
- 1 t thyme
- 1 bay leaf
- 1/2 t crushed red pepper
- 1 1/2 c chopped new potatoes
- 1 c carrots, sliced
- 1/2 c zucchini, chopped
- 1 c celery, sliced
- 1 (8 3/4 oz.) can corn, drained
- 2 to 3 c water
- 3 t chicken instant granules (low-salt)

Cook on low for 6 to 8 hours. Serves 12.

Calories per serving: 122

Carbohydrates:	15 g	Fiber:	3 g
Protein:	11 g	Sodium:	94 mg
		Cholesterol:	24 mg
Total Fat:	3 g		
Saturated Fat:	.6 g		
Monounsaturated Fat:	.8 g		

Calories from protein: 35%
Calories from carbohydrates: 47%
Calories from fats: 18%

Dijon Chicken

In pan sprayed with vegetable spray brown:
    1 lb. chicken breast, sliced

In saucepan add:
    1 c water
    3 T flour
    1 1/2 t low-sodium instant chicken bouillon
    1 T cornstarch

Stir until mixed. Add:
    1 c skim milk
    3 T chives
    2 T Dijon mustard

Pour mixture over chicken and cook; simmer for 10 to 15 minutes. Serve over 1/2 cup cooked brown rice. Serves 4.

Calories per serving: 320

Carbohydrates:	35	Fiber:	1.6 g
Protein:	32 g	Sodium:	200 mg
		Cholesterol:	73 mg
Total Fat:	5 g		
Saturated Fat:	1.3 g		
Monounsaturated Fat:	2 g		

Calories from protein: 41%
Calories from carbohydrates: 45%
Calories from fats: 14%

TANGY CHICKEN BREASTS

In medium airtight container combine:
- 2 T grated orange rind
- 1 t grated lemon rind
- 1 1/2 c orange juice, diluted
- 1/4 c lemon juice
- 1 t salt-free vegetable seasoning
- 1/2 t rosemary
- 2 T soy sauce (low-salt)

Mix well, then place in mixture:
- 1 lb. boneless, skinless chicken breast filets

Marinate for 2 to 3 hours. Place chicken with the marinade in a baking dish. Cover with foil and bake in oven at 400° for 25 to 35 minutes or until tender.

In small jar shake:
- 1 T skim milk
- 2 t cornstarch

In small saucepan pour 1 cup of the marinade and the cornstarch mixture. Cook over medium heat until sauce begins to thicken.

Cook and prepare according to box:
- 2 1/2 c cooked brown rice

Place rice on serving platter. Arrange chicken breasts on top of rice. Place orange slices on top of chicken. Pour sauce over entire dish. Serves 4.

(Continued Next Page)

Tangy Chicken Breasts

Calories per serving: 350

Carbohydrates: 45 g   Fiber: 2.4 g
Protein: 31 g   Sodium: 126 mg
Cholesterol: 72 mg
Total Fat: 5 g
Saturated Fat: 1.3 g
Monounsaturated Fat: 1.6 g

Calories from protein: 36%
Calories from carbohydrates: 52%
Calories from fats: 13%

BARBECUE TURKEY TATERS

In skillet sprayed with vegetable spray brown:
  1 lb. turkey breast slices
  1/2 med. purple onion, sliced very thin

Cook on medium-high for 5 minutes, turning turkey slices. Remove turkey slices and set aside. Add to skillet:
  2 c water
  3 med. new potatoes, sliced very thin
  1 t very low-sodium chicken broth granules

Boil, then reduce heat and cook for 15 minutes. Add:
  1/2 c barbecue sauce

Add turkey slices and simmer for 15 minutes. Serves 6.

Calories per serving: 166

Carbohydrates: 17 g   Fiber: 1 g
Protein: 19 g   Sodium: 233 mg
Cholesterol: 39 mg
Total Fat: 3 g
Saturated Fat: .7 g
Monounsaturated Fat: .5 g

Calories from protein: 46%
Calories from carbohydrates: 41%
Calories from fats: 14%

CREAMY TURKEY

In small jar with lid shake:
> 2 T unbleached flour
> 1 T cornstarch
> 1/4 c skim milk

In saucepan melt:
> 1 T diet margarine

Add:
> 1 3/4 c skim milk
> 1/8 t pepper
> 1/8 t salt

Stir and then gradually add the milk and flour mixture. Stir until thickened, then add:
> 1 c chopped turkey breast

Serve over whole wheat toast. Serves 6 (1/2 cup servings).

Calories per serving: 158

Carbohydrates: 20 g   Fiber: 2.5 g
Protein: 13 g   Sodium: 304 mg
Cholesterol: 17 mg
Total Fat: 3 g
Saturated Fat: 1 g
Monounsaturated Fat: 1 g

Calories from protein: 33%
Calories from carbohydrates: 50%
Calories from fats: 17%

PLUM-BARBECUED TURKEY TENDERLOINS

In skillet sprayed with vegetable spray brown:
    1 lb. turkey tenderloins

In food processor place:
    1 can (16 oz.) plums, drained and pitted
    1/4 c chopped onion
    1/4 c chili sauce
    2 T lemon juice
    1 T prepared mustard

Cover and blend on medium speed until well-blended.

Place tenderloins in 13 x 9 inch pan sprayed with vegetable spray. Pour plum mixture over turkey. Cover and bake at 350° for 15 minutes. Uncover and bake for an additional 10 minutes. Serves 6.

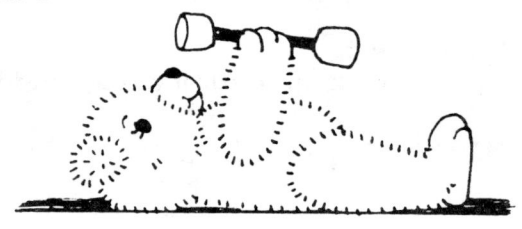

Calories per serving: 150

Carbohydrates:	15 g	Fiber:	1.4 g
Protein:	18 g	Sodium:	222 mg
		Cholesterol:	39 mg

Total Fat: 2 g
    Saturated Fat: .6 g
    Monounsaturated Fat: .4 g

Calories from protein: 47%
Calories from carbohydrates: 41%
Calories from fats: 12%

Mexican Turkey Dish

In skillet sprayed with vegetable spray sauté:
    1 lb. ground turkey breast
    1 med. onion, chopped
    1/4 t garlic powder
    1/4 t salt
    1/4 t cumin
    1/2 c celery, sliced

Cook until turkey is no longer pink. Stir in:
    1 (14 1/2 oz.) can stewed tomatoes (low-salt)
    1 (16 oz.) can kidney beans, drained and rinsed
    1 (4 oz.) can diced green chilies
    1 c frozen corn, thawed

Bring to boil. Reduce heat. Cover and simmer for 10 to 15 minutes. Stir in:
    3 c cooked elbow macaroni

Sprinkle with:
    1/4 c lowfat cheddar cheese, shredded

Serves 8.

Calories per serving: 258

    Carbohydrates: 36 g   Fiber: 7 g
    Protein: 22 g   Sodium: 145 mg
                               Cholesterol: 33 mg
    Total Fat: 3 g
        Saturated Fat: 1.3 g
        Monounsaturated Fat: .7 g

    Calories from protein: 34%
    Calories from carbohydrates: 54%
    Calories from fats: 12%

MOZZARELLA TURKEY SLICES

In shallow dish whip with fork:
> 2 egg whites
> 2 T water

In another shallow dish mix:
> 3/4 oat bran (unprocessed)
> 1 t garlic powder

Dip in egg mixture and then dredge through bran mixture:
> 1 lb. turkey breast slices (6 to 7 slices)

Spray skillet with vegetable spray. Brown each side of each slice. Arrange slices in casserole dish sprayed with vegetable spray.

Pour over slices:
> 1 (8 oz.) can tomato sauce
> (no salt added)

Sprinkle with:
> 1/4 c finely chopped parsley
> 1/3 c grated mozzarella cheese

Bake at 350° for 20 to 25 minutes. Serves 6.

Calories per serving: 200

Carbohydrates:	13 g	Fiber:	1.5 g
Protein:	25 g	Sodium:	159 mg
		Cholesterol:	47 mg
Total Fat:	5 g		
Saturated Fat:	2 g		
Monounsaturated Fat:	1 g		

Calories from protein: 50%
Calories from carbohydrates: 26%
Calories from fats: 23%

SPICY TURKEY SALAD

In bowl combine:
- 2 c cooked turkey, diced
- 1 c grated carrot
- 1/2 c finely chopped celery
- 1/3 c finely chopped red onion
- 1/2 c finely chopped tomatoes

In small bowl whip with whisk:
- 1/4 c Miracle Whip (fat-free)
- 3 T skim milk
- 1 T lemon juice
- 1/4 t crushed cumin
- 1/4 t chili powder
- 2 T cilantro leaves

Pour over turkey mixture. Toss until well-blended. Serve over lettuce. Serves 6.

Calories per serving: 111

Carbohydrates:	5 g	Fiber:	1 g
Protein:	14 g	Sodium:	80 mg
		Cholesterol:	37 mg
Total Fat:	3 g		
Saturated Fat:	1 g		
Monounsaturated Fat:	.8 g		

Calories from protein: 53%
Calories from carbohydrates: 19%
Calories from fats: 28%

TURKEY-APPLE PITA POCKETS

In bowl toss:
- 1 c turkey breast, cooked and chopped
- 1 c shredded cabbage
- 3/4 c apple, chopped
- 1/3 c grated nonfat cheddar cheese

In small bowl whisk:
- 1/4 c nonfat Miracle Whip
- 1 T plain nonfat yogurt
- 2 t mustard
- 1 T skim milk

Pour mixture over turkey mixture. Stir until well-coated. Spoon mixture into:
- 3 lg. whole wheat pita pockets, halved

Serves 6.

Calories per serving: 182

Carbohydrates: 21 g   Fiber: 1 g
Protein: 15 g   Sodium: 302 mg
Cholesterol: 25 mg
Total Fat: 4 g
Saturated Fat: 2 g
Monounsaturated Fat: 1 g

Calories from protein: 32%
Calories from carbohydrates: 47%
Calories from fats: 21%

Turkey Barbecue

In skillet place:
>1/2 c unsweetened pineapple juice
>2 T crushed pineapple (unsweetened)
>1 T honey
>1/2 c chopped onion
>1/3 c chopped green onion

Cook on medium for 5 minutes. Add:
>1 lb. ground turkey breast

Cook on medium-high until turkey is done. Add:
>1 (6 oz.) tomato paste (no salt added)
>1/2 c water
>2 t Dijon mustard
>1/2 t garlic powder

Stir. Simmer on low heat for 30 minutes. Serve on whole grain rolls. Serves 6.

Calories per serving: 146

Carbohydrates:	14 g	Fiber:	1 g
Protein:	19 g	Sodium:	77 mg
		Cholesterol:	39 mg
Total Fat:	2 g		
Saturated Fat:	.6 g		
Monounsaturated Fat:	.4 g		

Calories from protein: 50%
Calories from carbohydrates: 36%
Calories from fats: 13%

TURKEY BURGERS

In large bowl combine:
- 1 lb. ground turkey breast
- 1 egg white, whipped
- 1/4 c onion, finely chopped
- 1 t parsley
- 1/2 t salt-free seasoning
- 1/4 t pepper

Form 4 patties. Cook on grill or in pan sprayed with vegetable spray. Serves 4.

For additional flavor, add a little barbecue sauce.

Calories per serving: 142

Carbohydrates:	1 g	Fiber:	.3 g
Protein:	26 g	Sodium:	68 mg
		Cholesterol:	59 mg
Total Fat:	3 g		
Saturated Fat:	1 g		
Monounsaturated Fat:	.5 g		

Calories from protein: 78%
Calories from carbohydrates: 4%
Calories from fats: 18%

TURKEY OVER NOODLES

Shake in jar until dissolved:
    1/2 c skim milk
    2 T unbleached flour
    2 T cornstarch

Melt in saucepan:
    1 T diet margarine

Add milk mixture to saucepan. Stir, then add:
    1 1/2 c skim milk
    1 t chicken bouillon granules
      (low-salt)

Cook on medium heat until thick, then add:
    1 c chopped cooked turkey
    1 T chopped parsley
    1/2 c sm. cooked peas

Cook until completely heated. Serve over:
    4 c cooked pasta

Serves 6.

Calories per serving: 230

Carbohydrates:	36 g	Fiber:	1.4 g
Protein:	15 g	Sodium:	0 mg
		Cholesterol:	18 mg

Total Fat: 2 g
    Saturated Fat: .6 g
    Monounsaturated Fat: .6 g

Calories from protein: 27%
Calories from carbohydrates: 64%
Calories from fats: 9%

Turkey Potato Skins

Toss in small bowl:
    1/2 c grated mozzarella cheese
      (part skim)
    1/2 c lowfat cheddar
    2 T chives
    1/2 t salt-free Original Seasoning
    1/4 t garlic powder

Bake until fully cooked:
    5 med. potatoes

Slice potatoes in half. Spoon out potato, leaving the skins with just a little potato in each.

Divide evenly and spoon into each skin:
    1 c finely chopped cooked turkey breast

Top each half with cheese mixture. Bake at 400° for 10 minutes or until cheese is melted. Makes 10 skins.

Calories per serving: 143

Carbohydrates: 21 g   Fiber: 1.6 g
Protein: 9 g   Sodium: 76 mg
    Cholesterol: 16 mg
Total Fat: 2 g
Saturated Fat: 1.4 g
Monounsaturated Fat: .6 g

Calories from protein: 26%
Calories from carbohydrates: 59%
Calories from fats: 15%

TURKEY SLOPPY JOES

In skillet sprayed with vegetable spray brown:
- 1 lb. ground turkey breast
- 1/3 c chopped green onions
- 1/3 c chopped green pepper
- 1/2 c chopped tomatoes
- 1/4 t ginger
- 1 clove garlic, minced

Cook over medium heat until turkey is browned. Add:
- 3 T teriyaki sauce (low-salt)
- 2 t cider vinegar
- 1/3 c tomato paste
- 1/2 c water
- 1/3 c catsup

Simmer for 20 minutes. Add more water, if needed. Makes 3 1/2 cups. Serve on whole wheat buns. Serves 6.

Calories per serving: 131

Carbohydrates:	10 g	Fiber:	1 g
Protein:	18 g	Sodium:	404 mg
		Cholesterol:	39 mg
Total Fat:	2 g		
Saturated Fat:	.6 g		
Monounsaturated Fat:	.4 g		

Calories from protein: 57%
Calories from carbohydrates: 29%
Calories from fats: 14%

TURKEY SPAGHETTI SAUCE

In skillet sauté:
- 3/4 lb. ground turkey breast
- 1/4 c chopped green pepper
- 1/4 c chopped scallions
- 1/4 c chopped onion
- 1/2 t crushed garlic

Add:
- 2 (14 1/2 oz.) cans stewed tomatoes (no salt added)
- 1 (8 oz.) can tomato sauce
- 1 T Parsley Patch Salt-Free Italian Blend
- 1 t oregano
- 1/2 t basil
- 1 T parsley
- 1/2 t garlic powder

Simmer on low 20 to 30 minutes. Makes 5 cups. Serves 12.

Calories per serving: 132

Carbohydrates:	14 g	Fiber:	4.4 g
Protein:	16 g	Sodium:	343 mg
		Cholesterol:	31 mg
Total Fat:	2 g		
Saturated Fat:	.5 g		
Monounsaturated Fat:	.3 g		

Calories from protein: 47%
Calories from carbohydrates: 40%
Calories from fats: 13%

Turkey Tetrazzini

In skillet sprayed with vegetable spray add:
    1/2 c chopped onion
    1 T diet margarine
    1 T parsley

In small jar with lid shake until dissolved:
    1/4 c flour
    1 c skim milk

Add milk mixture to onion mixture. Stir and add:
    1 c skim milk
    1 t instant chicken bouillon granules (low-salt)

Stir until thickened, then add:
    1 1/2 c turkey breast, cooked and diced
    1/2 c sm. peas

In casserole dish (7 1/2 x 12 1/2 inch) place:
    3 c cooked spaghetti noodles (yolkless)

Pour turkey mixture over noodles. Sprinkle with:
    1/3 c bread crumbs
    1/2 t pepper
    1 T Parmesan cheese

Bake at 350° for 20 minutes, covered. Serves 10.

(Continued Next Page)

TURKEY TETRAZZINI (CONTINUED)

Calories per serving: 147

Carbohydrates: 21 g   Fiber: 1 g
Protein: 11 g   Sodium: 95 mg
Cholesterol: 16 mg
Total Fat: 2 g
Saturated Fat: .6 g
Monounsaturated Fat: .5 g

Calories from protein: 31%
Calories from carbohydrates: 57%
Calories from fats: 12%

TURKEY WITH APPLE SLICES

Cut into thin slices:
>1 lb. turkey breast, skinless

Sauté in skillet sprayed with vegetable spray. Brown slices on both sides.

Sprinkle with:
>1/2 t pepper
>1/2 t cajun spice
>1/2 t garlic powder

Cook on medium for 5 minutes. In small bowl combine:
>2 T apple juice, undiluted
>1 c water
>1/2 t chicken bouillon granules (low-salt)
>2 T applesauce

Pour over turkey. Then add:
>1 med. apple, sliced thinly

Simmer for 10 to 15 minutes or until tender. Serves 4.

Calories per serving: 164

Carbohydrates:	8 g	Fiber:	1.2 g
Protein:	26 g	Sodium:	100 mg
		Cholesterol:	59 mg
Total Fat:	3 g		
Saturated Fat:	1 g		
Monounsaturated Fat:	.5 g		

Calories from protein: 64%
Calories from carbohydrates: 19%
Calories from fats: 17%

TURKEY WITH DIJON SAUCE

In bowl mix:
- 1 lb. ground turkey breast
- 1 slice whole wheat bread, crumbled
- 1/4 c finely chopped onion
- 1/2 t pepper

Shape into 24 meatballs. Place in skillet sprayed with vegetable spray and cook, covered, for 15 to 20 minutes or until is cooked. Set aside. In saucepan combine:
- 3 T unbleached flour
- 1 T cornstarch
- 1 1/2 t chicken broth granules (low-sodium)
- 1 c water

Stir until dry ingredients are dissolved. Add:
- 1 c skim milk
- 3 T finely chopped chives
- 2 T Dijon mustard
- 1/4 t pepper
- 1 t lemon juice

Cook over medium heat until mixture thickens and boils, stirring constantly. Add meatballs to mixture, stirring gently, until meatballs are heated. Serve over:
- 3 c cooked noodles (yolkless)

Serves 6.

(Continued Next Page)

TURKEY WITH DIJON SAUCE (CONTINUED)
Calories per serving: 244

Carbohydrates: 28 g Fiber: 1.5 g
Protein: 23 g Sodium: 174 mg
Cholesterol: 30 mg
Total Fat: 4 g
Saturated Fat: 1 g
Monounsaturated Fat: 1 g

Calories from protein: 39%
Calories from carbohydrates: 48%
Calories from fats: 13%

PASTA, POTATOES & RICE

Fruit And Pasta

In small saucepan, with whisk beat until foamy:
> 3 egg whites

Add:
> 3 T pineapple juice, reserved from canned pineapple
> 3 T lemon juice
> 1 T sugar
> 1 T diet margarine

Cook over low heat until mixture thickens, stirring constantly for about 2 minutes. Cool to room temperature. In large bowl combine:
> 1 (11 oz.) can mandarin oranges, drained
> 1 c seedless grapes, halved
> 1 c miniature marshmallows
> 3 c cooked yolkless macaroni noodles

Mix well. Fold in egg white mixture. Add:
> 1 1/2 c Cool Whip Lite

Cover; chill thoroughly. Serves 10.

Calories per serving: 155

Carbohydrates:	29 g	Fiber:	1 g
Protein:	3 g	Sodium:	44 mg
		Cholesterol:	0 mg
Total Fat:	4 g		
Saturated Fat:	2.6 g		
Monounsaturated Fat:	.4 g		

Calories from protein: 7%
Calories from carbohydrates: 78%
Calories from fats: 20%

Mac And Cheese

Cook according to directions:
    8 oz. elbow macaroni (no yolk)

In saucepan combine:
    1 (16 oz.) can stewed tomatoes (no salt added)
    1 (6 oz.) can tomato paste (no salt added)
    1/2 c water
    1/2 c onion, chopped
    2 t salt-free Italian herb
    1/4 t garlic powder
    1/4 t black pepper

Bring to boil, then reduce heat and cook for 10 minutes.

Spray casserole dish with vegetable spray. Place half of the noodles on the bottom of the dish, then place half of the tomato mixture on top of the noodles. In small bowl combine:
    1 c skim milk ricotta cheese
    1 c (1%) cottage cheese
    2 T parsley, chopped

Place half of the cheese mixture on top of tomato mixture. Place remaining noodles, then the remaining cheese mixture and top with the remaining tomato mixture. On top sprinkle:
    1/4 c grated lowfat mozzarella cheese
    1 T grated Parmesan cheese

Bake at 375° for 30 to 35 minutes. Serves 6.

(Continued Next Page)

Mac And Cheese (Continued)

Calories per serving: 203

Carbohydrates:	23 g	Fiber:	3 g
Protein:	16 g	Sodium:	292 mg
		Cholesterol:	20 mg
Total Fat:	6 g		
Saturated Fat:	3.5 g		
Monounsaturated Fat:	2 g		

Calories from protein: 30%
Calories from carbohydrates: 44%
Calories from fats: 26%

MEXICAN PASTA SALAD

In bowl mix:
- 4 c cooked curly pasta
- 1/2 c salsa

Cool in refrigerator for 30 minutes, then add:
- 1 c salsa
- 3/4 c red onion, chopped
- 2 c tomato, chopped
- 1 c red pepper, chopped
- 1 c green pepper, chopped
- 1 c cooked black beans
- 1 c cooked corn
- 1 c jicama, diced
- 1 T cilantro

Mix thoroughly and refrigerate at least 1 hour before serving. Serves 14.

Calories per serving: 105

Carbohydrates:	20 g	Fiber:	3 g
Protein:	4 g	Sodium:	57 mg
		Cholesterol:	14 mg

Total Fat: 1.5 g
Saturated Fat: .3 g
Monounsaturated Fat: .7 g

Calories from protein: 15%
Calories from carbohydrates: 73%
Calories from fats: 12%

Quick Pasta Dish

In pie plate sprayed with vegetable spray place:
>3 c cooked spaghetti noodles, yolkless

In small saucepan heat:
>1 can (15 oz.) black beans with chili spices

On top of noodles spread:
>1 can (15 oz.) diced tomatoes

Pour over tomatoes the heated beans. On top, pour:
>1 can (8 oz.) tomato sauce (no salt added)

Sprinkle on top:
>1/2 c mozzarella cheese

Bake at 350° for 15 to 20 minutes, until thoroughly heated. Serves 6.

Calories per serving: 244

Carbohydrates: 44 g   Fiber: 9 g
Protein: 13 g   Sodium: 68 mg
Cholesterol: 5 mg
Total Fat: 2.5 g
Saturated Fat: 1.1 g
Monounsaturated Fat: .6 g

Calories from protein: 21%
Calories from carbohydrates: 70%
Calories from fats: 9%

Pasta And Vegetable Salad

In large bowl place:
    1 c chopped broccoli
    1 1/2 c sliced cauliflower
    1 c sliced fresh mushrooms
    1/2 c sliced zucchini
    1 c chopped tomatoes
    1 c chopped carrots
    1/2 c sliced green onions
    1/2 c chopped red pepper
    1/2 c chopped yellow pepper
    1/4 c chopped fresh parsley

Cook according to directions on package:
    1 (1 lb.) pkg. elbow macaroni (no yolk)

Rinse macaroni with cold water. Drain and then toss with vegetable mixture. Pour on top of mixture:
    1 c oil-free Italian dressing

Toss gently until well-blended. Cover; chill thoroughly. Serves 14.

Calories per serving: 115

Carbohydrates:	21 g	Fiber:	2 g
Protein:	4 g	Sodium:	144 mg
		Cholesterol:	1 mg
Total Fat:	1 g		
Saturated Fat:	.2 g		
Monounsaturated Fat:	.3 g		

Calories from protein: 13%
Calories from carbohydrates: 77%
Calories from fats: 10%

Pasta Salad

In bowl combine:
- 4 c cooked spiral pasta
- 1 c sliced carrots
- 1 c sliced celery
- 1 med. tomato, chopped
- 1/8 c chopped red pepper
- 1/8 c chopped black olives
- 1/4 c chopped red onion
- 1/2 c salsa (hot or mild)

Toss until well-blended. Serves 10.

Calories per serving: 97

Carbohydrates: 19 g   Fiber: 2 g
Protein: 3 g   Sodium: 48 mg
Cholesterol: 0 mg
Total Fat: 1 g
Saturated Fat: .2 g
Monounsaturated Fat: .5 g

Calories from protein: 13%
Calories from carbohydrates: 78%
Calories from fats: 10%

Poppy Seed Noodles

In large saucepan place:
>3 T light olive oil
>2 T poppy seeds

Cook for 3 minutes. Add:
>1/2 t salt
>1/2 t pepper
>1 t dried parsley

Cook for 1 minute. Add:
>4 c cooked yolkless wide noodles

Toss until noodles are heated through, about 2 to 3 minutes. Serves 6.

Calories per serving: 209

Carbohydrates:	26 g	Fiber:	1 g
Protein:	5 g	Sodium:	180 mg
		Cholesterol:	0 mg
Total Fat:	9 g		
Saturated Fat:	1.4 g		
Monounsaturated Fat:	5.6 g		

Calories from protein: 10%
Calories from carbohydrates: 50%
Calories from fats: 41%

Spaghetti Pie

In skillet sprayed with vegetable spray sauté:
> 3/4 lb. ground turkey breast
> 1/2 c chopped onion
> 1/2 c green pepper
> 1 t garlic powder

Cook until turkey is done. In small bowl whip:
> 1 egg
> 1 egg white
> 2 T Parmesan cheese, grated

Toss with:
> 14 oz. spaghetti noodles, cooked and drained

Press noodle mixture into large pie dish. Place turkey mixture on top of noodles. Sprinkle with:
> 1/4 c lowfat mozzarella cheese

Pour on top of cheese:
> 2 c prepared nonfat spaghetti sauce

Spread evenly. Sprinkle with
> 1/3 c lowfat mozzarella cheese

Bake at 350° for 30 to 35 minutes. Serves 8.

Calories per serving: 231

Carbohydrates: 23 g   Fiber: 1 g
Protein: 19 g   Sodium: 366 mg
     Cholesterol: 65 mg
Total Fat: 6 g
Saturated Fat: 3 g
Monounsaturated Fat: 2.6 g

Calories from protein: 32%
Calories from carbohydrates: 39%
Calories from fats: 22%

VEGGIE PASTA

In large bowl combine:
        1 c chopped broccoli
        1/2 c chopped red onion
        1 c chopped cauliflower
        1 c chopped carrots
        1 c chopped celery
        1/2 c chopped green pepper
        3 c Wheelie Medley pasta, cooked
        1/4 c sliced black olives

In small bowl whip with whisk:
        3 T skim milk
        1/4 c nonfat ranch dressing

Pour over pasta mixture. Toss until blended.

Refrigerate for 1 hour before serving. Serves 10.

Calories per serving: 87

Carbohydrates:	16 g	Fiber:	2 g
Protein:	3 g	Sodium:	65 mg
		Cholesterol:	< 1 mg
Total Fat:	2 g		
Saturated Fat:	.3 g		
Monounsaturated Fat:	.7 g		

Calories from protein: 13%
Calories from carbohydrates: 70%
Calories from fats: 17%

CHEESEY POTATO SKINS

Bake and cut in half:
    5 med. potatoes

Scoop potato out from each half and place potato in bowl. Add:
    1/2 c part-skim mozzarella cheese
    1/4 c lowfat ricotta cheese
    1 T lowfat sour cream
    1/4 c (1%) lowfat cottage cheese
    1/4 c scallions
    1/4 c chopped fresh parsley
    1/2 t salt-free seasoning

Mix thoroughly. Place filling on each skin. Place skins on cookie sheet sprayed with vegetable spray. Sprinkle with paprika. Bake at 400° for 10 minutes. Broil until tops are brown. Serves 5.

Calories per serving: 174

Carbohydrates:	29 g	Fiber:	2 g
Protein:	8 g	Sodium:	129 mg
		Cholesterol:	11 mg
Total Fat:	3 g		
Saturated Fat:	2 g		
Monounsaturated Fat:	1 g		

Calories from protein: 19%
Calories from carbohydrates: 65%
Calories from fats: 16%

HASHED BROWN QUICHE

Spray skillet with vegetable spray sauté:
    1 med. onion, finely chopped
    1 T canola oil

Cook until translucent. Add:
    5 med.-sized potatoes, scrubbed and shredded

Cover skillet and cook 5 to 7 minutes over low heat, stirring occasionally, until potatoes are slightly browned.

In small bowl whisk:
    3 egg whites
    1 (12 oz.) can skim evaporated milk
    1/2 t soy sauce
    1/2 t dry mustard
    1/2 t pepper

Blend until smooth. Remove potato mixture from skillet. Using spoon, press into pie plate. Press over bottom and up sides like pie crust. Pour egg mixture into crust. Sprinkle with:
    1/2 c lowfat cheddar cheese
    3 T chopped fresh parsley
    Paprika

Bake at 350° for 40 to 45 minutes, until filling is set. Cut into wedges. Serves 8.

(Continued Next Page)

HASHED BROWN QUICHE (CONTINUED)

Calories per serving: 234

Carbohydrates: 38 g   Fiber: 2.8 g
Protein: 12 g   Sodium: 174 mg
Cholesterol: 10 mg
Total Fat: 4 g
Saturated Fat: 2 g
Monounsaturated Fat: 2 g

Calories from protein: 20%
Calories from carbohydrates: 64%
Calories from fats: 16%

Potato Salad

Place in boiling water and cook until tender:
    4 med. potatoes, chopped with skin on

Drain, rinse with cold water and place in mixing bowl. Add:
    3 hard-boiled egg whites
    1/4 c finely chopped onion
    1 c chopped celery
    1 t parsley

In small bowl whip with whisk:
    2 T Miracle Whip (fat-free)
    1 t mustard
    3 T skim milk

Pour mixture over potato mixture. Mix until blended. Serves 6.

Calories per serving: 108

Carbohydrates: 21 g
Protein: 4 g
Fiber: 2 g
Sodium: 87 mg
Cholesterol: 1 mg
Total Fat: 1 g
Saturated Fat: .2 g
Monounsaturated Fat: .3 g

Calories from protein: 14%
Calories from carbohydrates: 76%
Calories from fats: 9%

POTATO VEGETABLE DISH

In pot of water bring to boil and cook until tender:
>3 lg. potatoes, unpeeled and diced

Drain and set aside. In skillet sprayed with vegetable spray place:
>3/4 c diced onions
>3/4 c diced green peppers
>3/4 c diced red peppers
>1/4 c water
>1/2 t beef broth (low-sodium)

Cook over medium heat for 4 to 5 minutes. Add:
>1 c corn (canned or thawed)

Cook for 1 minute. Add potato mixture. Cook for 1 minute. Toss with:
>1/2 t thyme
>1/2 t tarragon
>1/4 t pepper
>1/4 t salt
>2 T cilantro

Cook 5 more minutes. Serves 8.

Calories per serving: 102

Carbohydrates:	23 g	Fiber:	2.7 g
Protein:	3 g	Sodium:	122 mg
		Cholesterol:	0 mg
Total Fat:	<1 g		
Saturated Fat:	<1 g		
Monounsaturated Fat:	<1 g		

Calories from protein: 9%
Calories from carbohydrates: 87%
Calories from fats: 4%

STUFFED POTATOES

Bake until done:
    4 med. potatoes

Cut in half lengthwise and scoop out insides. Place in bowl. Add:
    1 c (1%) cottage cheese
    1/2 c nonfat cheddar cheese
    1/4 c chopped green onions
    3 T salsa

Stir until well-combined. Scoop potato mixture back into the potato skins. Place in baking dish and bake at 350° for 15 to 20 minutes. Serves 4.

Calories per serving: 348

Carbohydrates:	54 g	Fiber:	4 g
Protein:	20 g	Sodium:	408 mg
		Cholesterol:	18 mg

Total Fat: 6 g
    Saturated Fat: 3.5 g
    Monounsaturated Fat: 1.7 g

Calories from protein: 23%
Calories from carbohydrates: 62%
Calories from fats: 15%

Sweet Potato Dish

In large saucepan place:
- 4 med. fresh sweet potatoes, peeled and chopped into cubes
- 2 c carrots, sliced

Pour in 1 inch boiling water. Cover and cook over medium heat 15 to 20 minutes. Drain. Add:
- 2 c apples, diced
- 1/4 c orange juice, diluted
- 3 T honey
- 1/4 c crushed pineapple (unsweetened), drained
- 1/2 t cinnamon
- 1/4 t nutmeg

Cook, stirring often, for an additional 5 to 10 minutes or until apples are tender. Pour into serving dish. Sprinkle top lightly with:
- 1/2 t cinnamon
- 1 T brown sugar

Serves 8.

Calories per serving: 161

Carbohydrates:	39 g	Fiber:	4 g
Protein:	2 g	Sodium:	38 mg
		Cholesterol:	0 mg
Total Fat:	< 1 g		
Saturated Fat:	.1 g		
Monounsaturated Fat:	0 g		

Calories from protein: 4%
Calories from carbohydrates: 93%
Calories from fats: 3%

CAJUN RICE

In skillet cook:
>1 c tomato sauce (no salt added)
>1/2 c finely chopped celery
>1/2 c finely chopped green pepper
>1/4 c finely chopped onion
>1/2 t Tabasco sauce
>1/2 t Cajun Spice Mix (see below)
>1/2 t oregano

Cook over medium heat for 10 to 15 minutes. Add:
>2 c cooked brown rice

Continue to cook for 10 to 15 more minutes. Serves 8.

Calories per serving: 74

Carbohydrates:	16 g	Fiber:	1 g
Protein:	2 g	Sodium:	192 mg
		Cholesterol:	0 mg
Total Fat:	< 1 g		
Saturated Fat:	.1 g		
Monounsaturated Fat:	.1 g		

Calories from protein: 10%
Calories from carbohydrates: 85%
Calories from fats: 5%

(Continued Next Page)

Cajun Rice (Continued)

CAJUN SPICE MIX:
In container with lid combine:
- 1 T paprika
- 1 t salt
- 1 t onion powder
- 1 t garlic powder
- 1 t cayenne pepper
- 3/4 t white pepper
- 3/4 t black pepper
- 1/2 t oregano
- 1/2 t thyme

Place lid on and shake. Store, tightly covered. Serving size = 1/2 teaspoon.

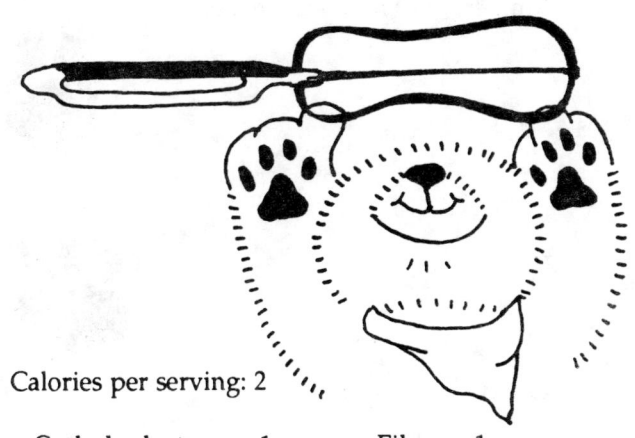

Calories per serving: 2

Carbohydrates: <1 g Fiber: .1 g
Protein: 0 g Sodium: 86 mg
Cholesterol: 0 mg
Total Fat: <1 g
Saturated Fat: 0 g
Monounsaturated Fat: 0 g

Calories from protein: 13%
Calories from carbohydrates: 65%
Calories from fats: 22%

FANCY RICE

In pan sprayed with vegetable spray sauté:
  1 c long grain rice, cooked
  1 c wild rice, cooked
  1/2 c chopped celery
  1/2 c chopped carrots
  1/4 c chopped onion
  1 T water

Cook for 5 minutes. Add:
  2 T soy sauce (low-salt)
  1/4 t cajun spice
  1 T water
  1/2 t cilantro leaves
  1 t chicken bouillon granules (low-salt)

Simmer for 10 minutes. Serves 6.

Calories per serving: 79

Carbohydrates: 17 g   Fiber: 1.5 g
Protein: 2 g   Sodium: 269 mg
Cholesterol: < 1 mg
Total Fat: < 1 g
Saturated Fat: 0 g
Monounsaturated Fat: 0 g

Calories from protein: 13%
Calories from carbohydrates: 85%
Calories from fats: 2%

LEMON RICE WITH PEAS

In saucepan bring to boil:
    2 1/4 c water

Add:
    3/4 c cooked instant brown rice

Cook for 2 to 3 minutes. Cover and set aside for 5 minutes.

Reduce heat to low. Stir in:
    5 lg. scallions, chopped
    3/4 c frozen peas, thawed
    1/2 t grated lemon peel

Cook on low for 3 to 5 minutes, until all ingredients are heated through. Serves 4.

Calories per serving: 163

    Carbohydrates: 34 g   Fiber: 3 g
    Protein: 5 g   Sodium: 33 mg
    Cholesterol: 0 mg
    Total Fat: <1 g
    Saturated Fat: .2 g
    Monounsaturated Fat: .2 g

    Calories from protein: 11%
    Calories from carbohydrates: 84%
    Calories from fats: 5%

RICE CASSEROLE

Spray casserole dish lightly with vegetable spray. Place in dish:
> 1 c sliced celery, thin slices
> 1/4 c chopped green pepper
> 1/4 c chopped red pepper
> 1/2 c chopped onion
> 1/2 t chopped garlic
> 1/4 c chopped parsley
> 1 c kidney beans, cooked
> 1 1/2 c brown rice, cooked
> 1 t salt-free seasoning
> 1 t Worcestershire sauce
> 1 c salt-free chicken broth

Mix until blended. Cover and bake at 350° for 25 minutes. Sprinkle with:
> 1/4 c lowfat mozzarella cheese

Broil until cheese has melted. Serves 10.

Calories per serving: 82

Carbohydrates: 13 g   Fiber: 2 g
Protein: 4 g   Sodium: 116 mg
Cholesterol: 3 mg
Total Fat: 1 g
Saturated Fat: .7 g
Monounsaturated Fat: .4 g

Calories from protein: 21%
Calories from carbohydrates: 64%
Calories from fats: 15%

WILD RICE

In skillet sauté:
- 1/4 c red onion
- 2 T red pepper, chopped
- 2 T green pepper, chopped
- 1 med. carrot, sliced thinly
- 1/2 tomato, chopped

Cook for 5 minutes. Add:
- 1/2 c water
- 2 T soy sauce (low-salt)
- 1 t chicken instant granules (low-salt)

Cook until vegetables are tender. Add:
- 1/4 c water
- 1 1/2 c cooked long grain wild rice mixture

Heat thoroughly and serve. Serves 6.

Calories per serving: 67

Carbohydrates: 14 g   Fiber: 1.6 g
Protein: 2 g   Sodium: 124 mg
                           Cholesterol: 0 mg
Total Fat: < 1 g
Saturated Fat: .1 g
Monounsaturated Fat: .1 g

Calories from protein: 12%
Calories from carbohydrates: 83%
Calories from fats: 4%

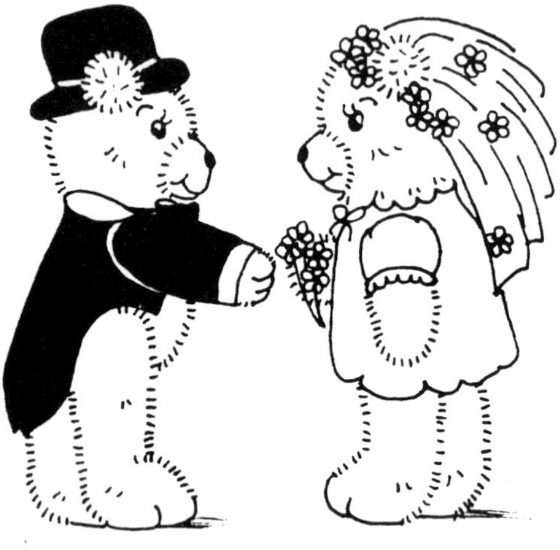

SALADS

APPLE-CHEESE SALAD

Halve and core:
    1 med. apple

Cut into 1/2 inch thick slices; cut slices into matchsticks. Sprinkle with lemon juice.

Cook, cool and cut into matchsticks:
    2 new potatoes

Also, cut into matchsticks:
    2 oz. hot pepper cheese

Combine all of the above into a large bowl.

In food processor place:
    1/4 c nonfat Miracle Whip
    4 T white wine vinegar
    1/4 t Dijon mustard
    2 T green onion, chopped
    1/8 t pepper

Whirl until well-blended. Add dressing to apple mixture. Toss gently to coat.

Arrange on serving platter:
    2 c shredded lettuce
    1 c shredded spinach leaves

(Continued Next Page)

Apple-Cheese Salad (Continued)

Calories per serving: 152

Carbohydrates: 25 g
Protein: 6 g
Total Fat: 3 g
Saturated Fat: 1.8 g
Monounsaturated Fat: .1 g
Fiber: 3.4 g
Sodium: 117 mg
Cholesterol: 9 mg

Calories from protein: 16%
Calories from carbohydrates: 64%
Calories from fats: 20%

A Taste Of Summer Salad

In large bowl combine:
- 2 c chopped cantaloupe
- 1 1/2 c blackberries, rinsed (whole)
- 2 c sliced strawberries
- 2 c sliced bananas
- 1 kiwi, sliced

Toss. In small bowl combine:
- 1/4 c frozen orange juice, undiluted
- 1/2 c plain nonfat yogurt

Pour over fruit. Chill. Makes 9 cups. Serves 18.

Calories per serving: 45

Carbohydrates: 11 g Fiber: 2 g
Protein: 1 g Sodium: 7 mg
Cholesterol: 0 mg
Total Fat: 0 g
Saturated Fat: 0 g
Monounsaturated Fat: 0 g

Calories from protein: 8%
Calories from carbohydrates: 87%
Calories from fats: 5%

BEAN, CORN AND PEPPER SALAD

In small bowl combine:
>   2 T apple juice, undiluted
>   1 T vinegar
>   3 T prepared salsa
>   1/4 t black pepper

In large bowl combine:
>   2 c canned black beans,
>   rinsed and drained
>   1 c canned corn, rinsed and drained
>   1/3 c red pepper, chopped
>   1/3 c green pepper, chopped
>   2 scallions, diced

Pour salsa mixture over bean mixture. Toss lightly. Chill for at least 1 hour before serving. Serve on lettuce leaves. Serves 8.

Calories per serving: 87

Carbohydrates:	17 g	Fiber:	5 g
Protein:	5 g	Sodium:	55 mg
		Cholesterol:	0 mg
Total Fat:	< 1 g		
Saturated Fat:	.1 g		
Monounsaturated Fat:	.2 g		

Calories from protein: 20%
Calories from carbohydrates: 74%
Calories from fats: 6%

Bean And Corn Salad

In large bowl combine:
- 1 1/2 c canned black beans, rinsed
- 1 1/2 c canned white Northern beans, rinsed
- 1 c canned corn, rinsed
- 1/3 c chopped green pepper
- 1/3 c chopped red onion
- 1 med. tomato, chopped
- 2 T apple juice concentrate
- 1 T vinegar
- 3 T salsa
- 1 T parsley
- 1/4 t black pepper

Toss well and chill for at least 1 hour. Serve on a bed of lettuce. Serves 8.

Calories per serving: 116

Carbohydrates:	22 g	Fiber:	6.7 g
Protein:	6 g	Sodium:	58 mg
		Cholesterol:	0 mg

Total Fat: 1 g
    Saturated Fat: .1 g
    Monounsaturated Fat: .2 g

Calories from protein: 21%
Calories from carbohydrates: 73%
Calories from fats: 6%

CARROT SALAD

In large bowl toss:
>3 c carrots, grated
>3/4 c raisins
>1 c crushed unsweetened pineapple, drained

In small bowl whisk:
>3 T nonfat Miracle Whip
>4 T skim milk

Whip until smooth and frothy. Pour over carrot mixture and toss until well-blended. Chill for 30 minutes. Serves 10.

Calories per serving: 72

Carbohydrates:	18 g	Fiber:	2 g
Protein:	1 g	Sodium:	24 mg
		Cholesterol:	0 mg
Total Fat:	< 1 g		
Saturated Fat:	.1 g		
Monounsaturated Fat:	.1 g		

Calories from protein: 5%
Calories from carbohydrates: 90%
Calories from fats: 5%

Colorful Slaw

In large bowl toss:
    1 c shredded red cabbage
    1 c shredded green cabbage
    1/2 c green pepper, diced
    1/2 c carrots, grated
    1/2 c sliced celery

In small bowl whisk:
    1 T nonfat yogurt
    2 T nonfat Miracle Whip
    1 T unsweetened apple juice, undiluted
    1/2 t Dijon mustard
    1/4 t ground pepper

Toss dressing and cabbage mixture. Chill for at least 30 minutes. Serves 4.

Calories per serving: 36

Carbohydrates:	7 g	Fiber:	1.7 g
Protein:	1 g	Sodium:	48 mg
		Cholesterol:	< 1 mg
Total Fat:	< 1 g		
Saturated Fat:	.1 g		
Monounsaturated Fat:	.2 g		

Calories from protein: 11%
Calories from carbohydrates: 72%
Calories from fats: 17%

COOKED CABBAGE

In skillet sprayed with vegetable spray sauté:
    1 T diet margarine
    2 T oil-free Italian dressing

Add:
    3 c shredded cabbage

Toss until well-coated. Sprinkle with:
    1/2 t salt
    1/2 t crushed caraway seeds
    1/4 t sugar
    1/4 t pepper

Cook 4 to 5 minutes or until cabbage is crisp-tender. Serves 6.

Calories per serving: 23

Carbohydrates: 2 g   Fiber: 1 g
Protein: < 1 g   Sodium: 246 mg
Cholesterol: 0 mg
Total Fat: 1 g
Saturated Fat: .2 g
Monounsaturated Fat: .5 g

Calories from protein: 9%
Calories from carbohydrates: 43%
Calories from fats: 48%

Cucumber Salad

In small bowl combine:
- 3/4 c rice wine vinegar
- 1 t dill weed
- 1 t sugar
- 1 t Mrs. Dash salt-free seasoning

In glass bowl place:
- 2 cucumbers, peeled, thinly sliced
- 1 med. red onion, thinly sliced

Pour vinegar mixture over cucumber/onion mixture. Chill for 1 hour. Serves 6.

Calories per serving: 23

Carbohydrates:	6g	Fiber:	1g
Protein:	<1g	Sodium:	3mg
		Cholesterol:	0mg

Total Fat: 0g
Saturated Fat: 0g
Monounsaturated Fat: 0g

Calories from protein: 10%
Calories from carbohydrates: 85%
Calories from fats: 5%

FANCY WALDORF SALAD

In small bowl whisk:
    1 T lemon juice
    1/4 c fat-free Miracle Whip
    2 T honey

In large bowl combine:
    1 c chopped red apples
    1 c chopped green apples
    3/4 c celery, diced
    3/4 c sliced green grapes
    1/3 c sliced almonds

Pour dressing over apple mixture. Toss lightly. Serves 8.

Calories per serving: 74

Carbohydrates:	13 g	Fiber:	1 g
Protein:	1 g	Sodium:	29 mg
		Cholesterol:	< 1 mg
Total Fat:	3 g		
Saturated Fat:	.3 g		
Monounsaturated Fat:	1.4 g		

Calories from protein: 5%
Calories from carbohydrates: 65%
Calories from fats: 31%

Fruity Slaw

In bowl combine:
- 3 c shredded green cabbage
- 3/4 c mandarin oranges, drained, reserving liquid
- 1/2 c chopped red apple
- 3 T crushed pineapple
- 1/2 c raisins
- 1 t celery seeds

In small bowl whip:
- 1/3 c nonfat yogurt
- 1/4 c fat-free Miracle Whip
- 1 t vanilla extract
- 2 T mandarin orange juice

Pour yogurt mixture over cabbage mixture. Stir until well-blended and refrigerate for 1 hour before serving. Serves 6.

Calories per serving: 113

Carbohydrates:	24 g	Fiber:	3 g
Protein:	2 g	Sodium:	70 mg
		Cholesterol:	3 mg
Total Fat:	2 g		
Saturated Fat:	.4 g		
Monounsaturated Fat:	.6 g		

Calories from protein: 6%
Calories from carbohydrates: 78%
Calories from fats: 16%

Hawaiian Waldorf Salad

In bowl add:
- 2 c unpeeled apple, chopped
- 1 c celery, sliced
- 1/2 c green grapes, sliced
- 1 c unsweetened pineapple tidbits, drained
- 2 T walnuts, chopped

In small bowl whip with whisk:
- 1 T lowfat yogurt
- 1 T fat-free Miracle Whip
- 1 T skim milk

Toss salad with dressing. Makes 4 cups. Serves 8.

Calories per serving: 66

Carbohydrates:	13 g	Fiber:	2 g
Protein:	1 g	Sodium:	26 mg
		Cholesterol:	< 1 mg
Total Fat:	2 g		
Saturated Fat:	.2 g		
Monounsaturated Fat:	.4 g		

Calories from protein: 4%
Calories from carbohydrates: 74%
Calories from fats: 22%

Mandarin Salad

Toss in large bowl:
>2 c finely chopped iceberg lettuce
>1 c finely chopped spinach
>1/2 c finely chopped carrots
>1/2 c chopped water chestnuts
>1 can (11 oz.) mandarin oranges, drained, reserving liquid

In small bowl mix:
>1/4 c mandarin orange juice
>1/4 c orange juice, diluted

Toss salad with juice just before serving. Serves 6.

Calories per serving: 51

Carbohydrates: 13 g
Protein: 1 g
Fiber: 2 g
Sodium: 16 g
Cholesterol: 0 mg
Total Fat: 0 g
Saturated Fat: 0 g
Monounsaturated Fat: 0 g

Calories from protein: 7%
Calories from carbohydrates: 91%
Calories from fats: 2%

ORANGE-BEET SALAD

In small bowl whisk:
    1/4 c orange juice, diluted
    1 T fat-free Italian dressing
    1/4 t lemon juice
    1/8 t pepper
    1/8 t salt

Arrange on large platter:
    4 c shredded lettuce

On top of lettuce arrange:
    1/2 lb. beets, cooked and peeled
    2 oranges, peeled and sectioned

Drizzle dressing over fruit and lettuce. Serves 6.

Calories per serving: 38

Carbohydrates:	8 g	Fiber:	2 g
Protein:	1 g	Sodium:	86 mg
		Cholesterol:	0 mg
Total Fat:	< 1 g		
Saturated Fat:	0 g		
Monounsaturated Fat:	.1 g		

Calories from protein: 12%
Calories from carbohydrates: 83%
Calories from fats: 6%

ORANGE CUCUMBER SALAD

In bowl place:
    1 1/2 c cucumber, thinly sliced

Sprinkle with:
    1/4 t salt
    1/4 t pepper

Toss with:
    1/2 c green pepper, chopped
    2 T fresh parsley, chopped
    2 med oranges, peeled and sectioned

In small bowl whisk:
    1/4 c nonfat plain yogurt
    2 T skim milk
    1/4 t thyme

Pour dressing over cucumber mixture and toss lightly. Cover and chill. Serve on lettuce. Serves 4.

Calories per serving: 52

    Carbohydrates: 12 g   Fiber: 2.2 g
    Protein: 2 g   Sodium: 150 mg
    Cholesterol: < 1 mg
    Total Fat: < 1 g
    Saturated Fat: .1 g
    Monounsaturated Fat: 0 g

    Calories from protein: 15%
    Calories from carbohydrates: 81%
    Calories from fats: 4%

Salad – Not Just Greens

In large bowl toss:
    2 c red leaf lettuce, torn into pieces
    1 c thinly sliced radishes
    1 c cucumber, thinly sliced
    1/2 c alfalfa sprouts
    1 c green pepper, thinly sliced
    1/2 c red onion, thinly sliced

In small bowl mix:
    1/2 c oil-free ranch dressing
    1/4 c chopped fresh parsley
    1 t lemon juice
    1/2 t dried oregano
    1/2 t dried mint leaves
    1/4 t ground cumin seed
    2 T skim milk

Whisk until smooth and frothy. Pour over greens and toss. Serves 6.

Calories per serving: 39

Carbohydrates:	5 g	Fiber:	1 g
Protein:	1 g	Sodium:	166 mg
		Cholesterol:	1 mg
Total Fat:	1 g		
Saturated Fat:	.1 g		
Monounsaturated Fat:	.4 g		

Calories from protein: 10%
Calories from carbohydrates: 47%
Calories from fats: 26%

TOMATO AND RICE SALAD

In bowl combine:
      3 c cooked brown rice, chilled
      3 med. tomatoes, chopped
      1 green pepper, chopped
      1/2 med. red onion, chopped
      2 T basil

In small bowl combine:
      1 T red wine vinegar
      1 T soy sauce (low-salt)
      2 T no oil Italian dressing

Pour dressing over rice mixture. Chill for at least an hour before serving. Serves 8.

Calories per serving: 112

Carbohydrates:	23 g	Fiber:	2 g
Protein:	3 g	Sodium:	98 mg
		Cholesterol:	0 mg
Total Fat:	< 1 g		
Saturated Fat	.2 g		
Monounsaturated Fat:	.2 g		

Calories from protein: 10%
Calories from carbohydrates: 83%
Calories from fats: 7%

Waldorf Salad

In bowl combine:
- 2 med. apples, chopped
- 1 c chopped celery
- 2 T chopped walnuts

In small bowl, with whisk, whip:
- 2 T Miracle Whip (fat-free)
- 1/4 c skim milk
- 1 t lemon juice

Pour over apple mixture and mix well. Serves 6.

Calories per serving: 54

Carbohydrates:	9 g	Fiber:	2 g
Protein:	1 g	Sodium:	32 mg
		Cholesterol:	< 1 mg
Total Fat:	2 g		
Saturated Fat:	.2 g		
Monounsaturated Fat:	.5 g		

Calories from protein: 6%
Calories from carbohydrates: 61%
Calories from fats: 32%

INDEX

BEANS AND SOUPS --- 1-16
- Baked Beans --------------------------- 1
- Baked Beans with Apple -------------- 2
- Black Bean Chili ---------------------- 3
- Black Bean and Rice Salad ----------- 4
- Anasazi Bean Soup -------------------- 5
- Black Bean Soup ---------------------- 6
- Chicken Noodle Soup ----------------- 7
- French Onion Soup -------------------- 8
- Gazpacho ---------------------------- 10
- Mexican Bean Soup ------------------ 11
- Pea Soup ---------------------------- 12
- Potato Soup ------------------------- 13
- Quick Soup -------------------------- 14
- Vegetable Barley Soup --------------- 15

BREADS AND MUFFINS ----------------------------------- 17-36
- Cherry Banana Bread ---------------- 17
- Cranberry Bread --------------------- 18
- Easy Raisin Bread ------------------- 19
- Jalapeno Corn Bread ---------------- 20
- Pumpkin Bread ---------------------- 21
- Pumpkin Date Bread ----------------- 22
- Banana Blueberry Muffins ----------- 23
- Banana Oatmeal Muffins ------------ 24
- Banana Raisin Nut Muffins ---------- 25
- Blueberry Muffins ------------------- 26
- Carrot Muffins ---------------------- 27
- Mandarin Orange Muffins ----------- 28
- Orange-Raspberry Muffins ---------- 29
- Pineapple Muffins ------------------- 30
- Pumpkin Muffins -------------------- 31
- Tangerine Muffins ------------------ 32
- Applesauce Rolls -------------------- 33
- Biscuits ------------------------------ 34
- Oat Bran Biscuits ------------------- 35
- Quick Biscuits ----------------------- 36

DESSERTS -- 37-66
- Apple-Butterscotch Bars ------------ 37
- Apple Tart --------------------------- 38

(Continued Next Page)

DESSERTS (CONTINUED)

Banana Cream Pie --- 40
Banana Orange Cookies --- 42
Banana Pudding Pie --- 44
Buttermilk-Cinnamon Coffee Cake --- 45
Chewy Date Bars --- 46
Chocolate-Amaretto Cheesecake --- 47
Hershey's Fudge Cake --- 48
Instant Sorbet --- 50
Jell-O Cake --- 51
Microwave Caramel Corn --- 53
Oatmeal Cookies --- 54
Oatmeal Butterscotch Cookies --- 55
Orange-Oat-Choc Cookies --- 56
Peach Cobbler --- 57
Peanut Butter Cookies --- 58
Pumpkin Chiffon Pie --- 59
Quick Pudding Delight --- 61
Raisin Bars --- 62
Raspberry Freeze --- 64
Strawberry Angel Squares --- 65

DIPS, DRESSING AND SAUCES --- 67-80

Cheddar Cheese Spread --- 67
Cucumber-Mustard Dip --- 68
Spinach Dip --- 69
Vegetable Dip --- 70
Bleu Cheese Dressing --- 71
Creamy Dressing --- 72
Creamy Garlic Dressing --- 73
Lemon Basil Salad Dressing --- 74
Orange Dressing --- 75
Salad Dressing --- 76
Blueberry Sauce --- 77
Marinara Sauce --- 78
Mexican Sauce --- 79
Papaya Marinade --- 80

EXTRAS --- 81-102

Butter – Extended --- 81
Cinnamon Apple Oatmeal --- 82
Fresh Salsa --- 83

(Continued Next Page)

EXTRAS (CONTINUED)

- Ginger Pancakes — 84
- Glazed Apples — 85
- Goulash — 86
- Herbed Carrots — 87
- Parmesan Crisps — 88
- Pizza Roll — 89
- Spicy Tomato Sauce — 91
- Stuffed Red Peppers — 92
- Tangy French Toast — 93
- Vegetable Casserole — 94
- Vegetable Pizza — 95
- Zucchini Tomato Bake — 97
- Hot Cranberry Sipper — 98
- Marmalade Tea — 99
- Orange Wassail — 100
- Punch — 101

FISH AND POULTRY — 103-142

- Easy Halibut — 103
- Grilled Shark — 104
- Halibut — 105
- Salmon Loaf — 106
- Salmon Pasta — 107
- Salmon Steaks — 108
- Tuna Potato Dish — 109
- Tuna Stir-Fry — 111
- Tuna-Topped Bagels — 112
- Apple-Honey Chicken — 113
- Breaded Chicken Breasts — 115
- Cajun Chicken and Rice — 116
- Chicken Fajitas — 117
- Chicken/Mandarin Salad — 119
- Chicken Salad — 120
- Chicken Stew — 121
- Dijon Chicken — 122
- Tangy Chicken Breasts — 123
- Barbecue Turkey Taters — 125
- Creamy Turkey — 126
- Plum-Barbecued Turkey Tenderloins — 127
- Mexican Turkey Dish — 128

(Continued Next Page)

FISH AND POULTRY (CONTINUED)

Mozzarella Turkey Slices------------129
Spicy Turkey Salad------------------130
Turkey-Apple Pita Pockets----------131
Turkey Barbecue---------------------132
Turkey Burgers-----------------------133
Turkey Over Noodles ----------------134
Turkey Potato Skins------------------135
Turkey Sloppy Joes-------------------136
Turkey Spaghetti Sauce -------------137
Turkey Tetrazzini--------------------138
Turkey with Apple Slices -----------140
Turkey with Dijon Sauce-------------141

PASTA, POTATOES AND RICE -----------------------------143-166

Fruit and Pasta-----------------------143
Mac and Cheese ----------------------144
Mexican Pasta Salad-----------------146
Quick Pasta Dish---------------------147
Pasta and Vegetable Salad----------148
Pasta Salad---------------------------149
Poppy Seed Noodles -----------------150
Spaghetti Pie------------------------151
Veggie Pasta-------------------------152
Cheesey Potato Skins ----------------153
Hashed Brown Quiche---------------154
Potato Salad-------------------------156
Potato Vegetable Dish---------------157
Stuffed Potatoes---------------------158
Sweet Potato Dish -------------------159
Cajun Rice----------------------------160
Fancy Rice ---------------------------162
Lemon Rice with Peas----------------163
Rice Casserole-----------------------164
Wild Rice----------------------------165

SALADS--167-184

Apple-Cheese Salad-----------------167
A Taste of Summer Salad ------------169
Bean, Corn and Pepper Salad--------170
Bean and Corn Salad-----------------171
Carrot Salad-------------------------172

(Continued Next Page)

SALADS (CONTINUED)

Colorful Slaw --------------------------- 173
Cooked Cabbage --------------------- 174
Cucumber Salad --------------------- 175
Fancy Waldorf Salad ---------------- 176
Fruity Slaw -------------------------- 177
Hawaiian Waldorf Salad ----------- 178
Mandarin Salad --------------------- 179
Orange-Beet Salad ------------------ 180
Orange Cucumber Salad ------------ 181
Salad – Not Just Greens ------------- 182
Tomato and Rice Salad ------------- 183
Waldorf Salad ---------------------- 184

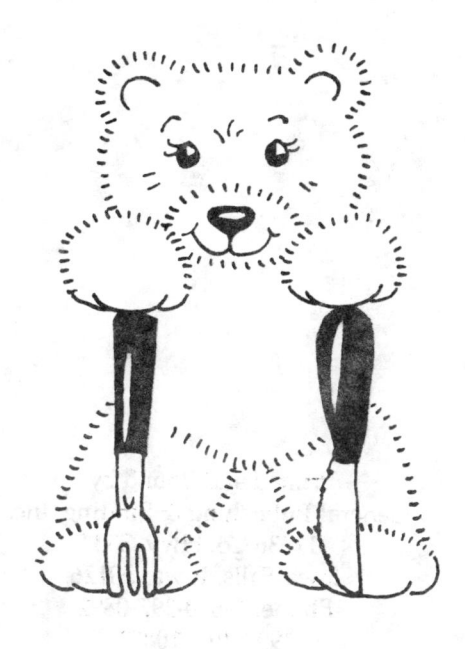

Printed and Bound by:
General Publishing & Binding, Inc.
11636 Co. Hwy. S33
Iowa Falls, Iowa 50126
Phone: 1-800-397-0892
1993 llw 10802

ORDER FORM

To order your copy or copies of "Bearly Any Fat" or "Bearly Any Fat Too" simply fill out the following form and mail to:

"Bearly Any Fat"
P.O. Box 5145
Wheatridge, CO 80034-5145

"Bearly Any Fat" — _____
  (number of books) @ $9.95

"Bearly Any Fat Too" — _____
  (number of books) @ $9.95

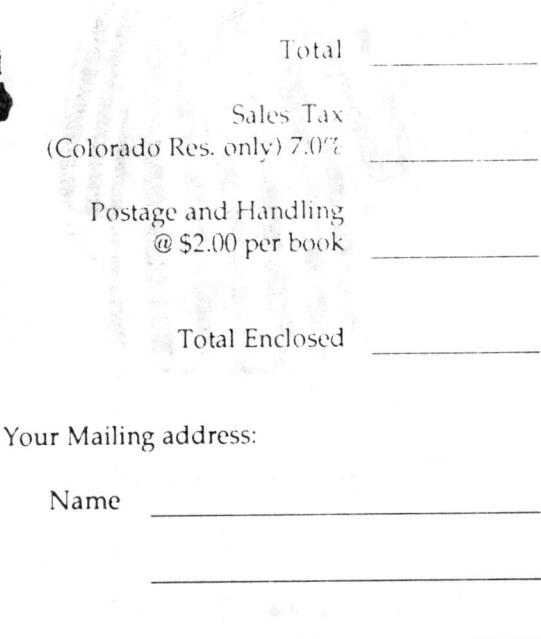

Total _____

Sales Tax
(Colorado Res. only) 7.0% _____

Postage and Handling
@ $2.00 per book _____

Total Enclosed _____

Your Mailing address:

Name _____

_____

_____

Please allow 2 to 4 weeks for delivery. Please enclose check made payable to "Bearly Any Fat".

THANK YOU!!!!!!   ENJOY!!!!!!

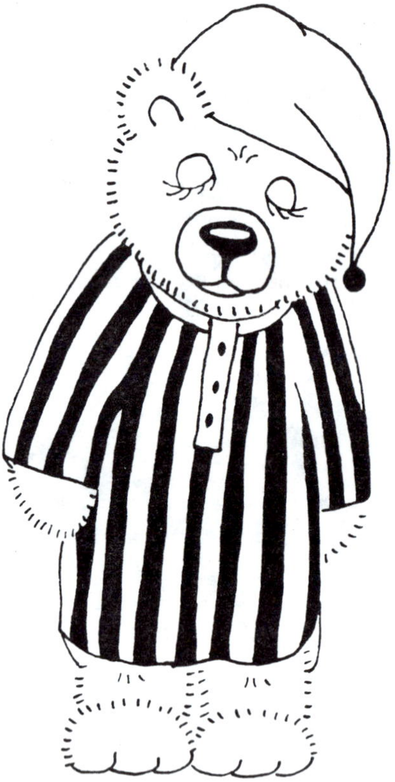